# PRESS ON

## 52 reasons to stay in the race

### A weekly devotional for Christian workers

## Richard Raher

**PRESS ON PUBLISHING**
Escondido, California

*Press On: 52 Reasons to Stay in the Race*
Copyright 2007, Richard R. Raher

All rights reserved.
No part of this publication may be reproduced in any
form without prior permission, except as
provided by USA copyright law.

Published by *Press On Publishing*
1742 El Aire Place
Escondido, CA 92026

All Scripture quotations in this book are
taken from the New King James Version.
Copyright 1982, Thomas Nelson, Inc.

Printed in the United States of America
ISBN 978-1-4243-4357-7

Cover Art: *Tim Arnold*

# ACKNOWLEDGEMENTS

This book could not have been written without the faithful encouragement and example of several pastors. These men have had their hands to the plow and have cared for their flocks faithfully for decades. I want to thank: Mike MacIntosh for introducing me to Jesus Christ and allowing me to serve, and make mistakes. Chuck Smith for his consistent availability, humble heart and strong exhortations to all of us younger pastors.

Jim Hesterly, who saw God's hand upon me and brought me into full time ministry. Pat Kenney, for his friendship to me and for bringing me on staff to serve the body at Calvary Chapel of Escondido. Rob Hubbard for heeding the call of God and caring for the body of Calvary Chapel Ramona.

Thanks to Jennie Gillespie and Michelle Striler for their editing gifts and prayers that this book would be a blessing to many. Love and thanks to the Lord for my best friend and faithful wife, Robbi, who constantly encourages me.

Richard R. Raher

iv    *Press On: 52 Reasons to Stay in the Race*

# FOREWORD

As a private pilot, I learned from the very beginning of my flight training in 1966 some important lessons that have kept me safe and brought much enjoyment and satisfaction from this wonderful area of my life. No lesson could be any more important than to have a map, and know where your destination is located, in relation to your departure site.

Richard Raher has very studiously laid out a 52-week devotional for us, his readers. Each week you can plot your course in the Bible, mix it with practical experience, and Richard's warm and lively insights. I can guarantee you will arrive at your destination much refreshed in one year.

Richard's friend,
Mike MacIntosh

*Press On: 52 Reasons to Stay in the Race*

# CONTENTS

INTRODUCTION . . . . . . . . . . . . . . . . . . . . . .XI

WEEK ONE: CALL OF GOD, NOAH . . . . . . . . . . . . . . . .1
Learning to Wait and Obey

WEEK TWO: VISION . . . . . . . . . . . . . . . . . . . . . .5
Believing the Lord Can Use You

WEEK THREE: FAITHFULNESS OF GOD . . . . . . . . . . . .7
A Valuable Lesson in Spiritual Labor

WEEK FOUR: PERSEVERANCE . . . . . . . . . . . . . . . . .9
Blood, Sweat, and Hot Metal

WEEK FIVE: REALITY OF GOD . . . . . . . . . . . . . . . .11
In Whom Do I Believe?

WEEK SIX: ANSWERS TO PRAYER . . . . . . . . . . . . . .13
Ask For Everything

WEEK SEVEN: FINISHING WELL . . . . . . . . . . . . . . .15
Exercising Godliness

WEEK EIGHT: CALL OF GOD, MOSES . . . . . . . . . . .17
Are You Talking to Me?

WEEK NINE: VISION . . . . . . . . . . . . . . . . . . . . .21
Reflection of God's Face

WEEK TEN: FAITHFULNESS OF GOD . . . . . . . . . . . . .23
When Common Sense Doesn't Matter

WEEK ELEVEN: PERSEVERANCE . . . . . . . . . . . . . . .27
The Making of the Valiant

WEEK TWELVE: REALITY OF GOD . . . . . . . . . . . . . .31
Simple Yet Profound

WEEK THIRTEEN: ANSWERS TO PRAYER . . . . . . . . . . .35
Eternal Perspective

WEEK FOURTEEN: FINISHING WELL . . . . . . . . . . . . .39
Addicted to Ministry

vii

WEEK FIFTEEN: CALL OF GOD, ABRAHAM . . . . . . . . . .41
"I Will"

WEEK SIXTEEN: VISION . . . . . . . . . . . . . . . . . . . .45
Lord, They Don't Understand

WEEK SEVENTEEN: FAITHFULNESS OF GOD . . . . . . . . .49
Help Me With My Unbelief

WEEK EIGHTEEN: PERSEVERANCE . . . . . . . . . . . . . .51
The Blessings of Old Age

WEEK NINETEEN: REALITY OF GOD . . . . . . . . . . . . . .55
Learning to Let Go

WEEK TWENTY: ANSWERS TO PRAYER . . . . . . . . . . . .59
Lord, I Need to Hear From You

WEEK TWENTY-ONE: FINISHING WELL . . . . . . . . . . . .61
Crossing the Finish Line

WEEK TWENTY-TWO: CALL OF GOD, GIDEON . . . . . . .63
Courage Under Fire

WEEK TWENTY-THREE: VISION . . . . . . . . . . . . . . . .67
Responding to Spiritual Needs

WEEK TWENTY-FOUR: FAITHFULNESS OF GOD . . . . . . .71
God Forgets My Sin But Remembers Me

WEEK TWENTY-FIVE: PERSEVERANCE . . . . . . . . . . . .75
Keeping a Promise to a Friend

WEEK TWENTY-SIX: REALITY OF GOD . . . . . . . . . . . .79
Seeing Jesus Through the Eyes of Paul

WEEK TWENTY-SEVEN: ANSWERS TO PRAYER . . . . . . .81
Wide Awake and Free!

WEEK TWENTY-EIGHT: FINISHING WELL . . . . . . . . . . .85
Leadership in Action

WEEK TWENTY-NINE: CALL OF GOD, PETER . . . . . . . .87
Fisherman to Fisher of Men

WEEK THIRTY: VISION . . . . . . . . . . . . . . . . . . . . . .91
Blessed Are the Eyes That See the Things You See

WEEK THIRTY-ONE: FAITHFULNESS OF GOD . . . . . . . .95
According to His Riches

WEEK THIRTY-TWO: PERSEVERANCE . . . . . . . . . . . . .99
"What Have I Done to You?"

WEEK THIRTY-THREE: REALITY OF GOD . . . . . . . . . .103
That Your Joy May Be Full

WEEK THIRTY-FOUR: ANSWERS TO PRAYER . . . . . . . .107
The Lord Always Listens

viii   *Press On: 52 Reasons to Stay in the Race*

WEEK THIRTY-FIVE: FINISHING WELL . . . . . . . . . . . . 111
Grow in Grace and Knowledge

WEEK THIRTY-SIX: CALL OF GOD, PAUL . . . . . . . . . 115
"Who Are You, Lord?"

WEEK THIRTY-SEVEN: VISION . . . . . . . . . . . . . . . . 119
Four Young Men of Passion

WEEK THIRTY-EIGHT: FAITHFULNESS OF GOD . . . . . . 123
Coming Back to Grace

WEEK THIRTY-NINE: PERSEVERANCE . . . . . . . . . . . 127
Enjoying the Ride

WEEK FORTY: REALITY OF GOD . . . . . . . . . . . . . . 131
When I Put My Hands in His Wounds

WEEK FORTY-ONE: ANSWERS TO PRAYER . . . . . . . . 135
Outnumbered and Outgunned

WEEK FORTY-TWO: FINISHING WELL . . . . . . . . . . . 139
When the Lord Rejoices

WEEK FORTY-THREE: CALL OF GOD, TIMOTHY . . . . . 141
Who Is the Paul in Your Life?

WEEK FORTY-FOUR: VISION . . . . . . . . . . . . . . . . 145
Answered Prayer from a Helpless Vessel

WEEK FORTY-FIVE: FAITHFULNESS OF GOD . . . . . . . 149
Washed and Set Apart for His Use

WEEK FORTY-SIX: PERSEVERANCE . . . . . . . . . . . . 151
When the Righteous Suffer

WEEK FORTY-SEVEN: REALITY OF GOD . . . . . . . . . .155
Remembering the Promise of God

WEEK FORTY-EIGHT: ANSWERS TO PRAYER . . . . . . . . 159
Why We Build Memorials

WEEK FORTY-NINE: FINISHING WELL . . . . . . . . . . 163
Young and in Captivity

WEEK FIFTY: FAITHFULNESS OF GOD . . . . . . . . . . . 167
"I Know You by Name"

WEEK FIFTY-ONE: ANSWERS TO PRAYER . . . . . . . . .171
Trusting in the Mercy of God

WEEK FIFTY-TWO: LIVING IN VICTORY! . . . . . . . . . .173

EPILOGUE . . . . . . . . . . . . . . . . . . . . . . . . . . .175

FOOTNOTES . . . . . . . . . . . . . . . . . . . . . . . . . .177

x    *Press On: 52 Reasons to Stay in the Race*

# INTRODUCTION

Monday mornings can be hard – especially for someone in fulltime ministry. Weekends are when our ministries are most seen by the public, when hours of preparing everything from sermons to Sunday school rooms comes under scrutiny, criticism, and heavy spiritual attack. On Monday morning many a battle weary servant wakes up feeling exhausted, alone, inadequate, and ready to quit. But before making such a drastic move, most of these servants will slide to their knees, pull out their Bibles, and pray for the strength to carry on.

This is a Monday morning devotional dedicated to those men and women serving God in full time ministry—those who have responded to the call of God, offering themselves as a living sacrifice in service to the Body of Christ. These servants face unique challenges and need specific kinds of encouragement and support. As someone who has worked in full time ministry for almost 30 years, I know. I also know the joy of being totally dedicated to the Kingdom and watching lives changed—and how inevitably this calling provokes spiritual warfare.

When we received Christ and salvation, Satan lost his dominion over us. We escaped his grasp and are destined for Heaven. That angers the enemy—a lot. It is one thing to escape his clutches yourself—and quite another to lead *others* to freedom as well.

We have an enemy in Satan who makes a concentrated effort to render God's servants barren and unfruitful. He simply wants to discourage us so deeply that we'll quit the ministry, and he'll use every conceivable tactic to prey upon our insecurities and faults. He'll exploit the weakness of our flesh, he'll try to puff up our pride, and he will gnaw away at our peace of mind with the cares of the world. He causes us to look at the rubble around us, to fix our gaze on the size of our adversaries, to look inward at our faults, and to become immobilized through discouragement.

A servant of the Lord often experiences his or her deepest depression and discouragement after a great victory. Elijah is a poignant example. He had just challenged the prophets of Baal, and called fire down from Heaven, which caused his people to fall on their faces saying, "The Lord is God! The Lord, He is God!" Then Elijah prophesied to the king, and witnessed the downpour of a miraculous rain. It was a moment of great spiritual victory!

Almost immediately afterward, Elijah fell into a deep depression in which he despaired of his own life. He was tired, hungry, and felt alone. He sat under a tree and cried, "Now, Lord, take my life..." (1 Kings 18-19).

That was Elijah's "Monday morning," and why this devotional is designed to be read the day after Sunday, usually your most demanding day of ministry. Monday is also the beginning of a new week of challenges, which often start the moment you get up. God spoke to Elijah in his moments of despair. He sent an angel to reassure him, reminding him that he was not alone, and then the Lord instructed Elijah on exactly what he was supposed to do next.

***This devotion is written to encourage and assist those who are being used by God to set others free.*** My prayer is that it will help you hear God speak, feel His presence, and keep your eyes on the Lord who called you. I pray that He will revive you, refresh you, and encourage you to stay in the fight and finish well.

There are seven main topics in this devotional, all directly related to the ministry: *the Call of God, Vision, the Faithfulness of God, Perseverance, Reality of God, Answers to Prayer,* and *Finishing Well.* You will go through a section of Scripture for each topic. The topics will repeat every seven weeks, for 52 weeks. You will need your Bible; although the weekly verses are included in the text with each devotion, it will be helpful for you to become familiar with them in context. My hope is that these Scriptures will be impressed upon your heart and become a part of you in the years ahead. Please write in your Bible, underline, and make notes in the text as you read weekly.

My prayer for you is the same as Paul the apostle wrote in his letter to the Church in Colosse: *"...that you may be filled with the knowledge of His will in all wisdom and spiritual understanding; that you may walk worthy of the Lord, fully pleasing Him, being fruitful in every good work and increasing in the knowledge of God; strengthened with all might, according to His glorious power, for all patience and longsuffering with joy; giving thanks to the Father who has qualified us to be partakers of the inheritance of the saints in the light"* (Colossians 1:9-12).

*Pastor Richard Raher*
Escondido, California

# WEEK ONE
## *Learning to Wait and Obey*

---

### *Call of God, Noah*

---

*But Noah found grace in the eyes of the Lord. This is the genealogy of Noah. Noah was a just man, perfect in his generations. Noah walked with God. And Noah begot three sons: Shem, Ham, and Japheth.*
— **Genesis 6:8-10**

Sometimes we forget that Noah was not in the ministry. Noah was a regular guy who kept his faith intact in the midst of an evil and totally depraved society. He had no fellowship with other believers, and no church to attend. His testimony was simple. He was a just man, "perfect in his generations," and he walked with God—not in the flow of society around him.

God's call upon his life was unique and in line with his natural abilities—which is how God works in our lives. He calls upon us to do His bidding with abilities He has given us, but He also calls upon us to become what He intends us to be. Os Guinness defines God's call upon our lives this way: "Calling is the truth that God calls us to Himself so decisively that everything we are, everything we do, and everything we have is invested with a special devotion, dynamism, and direction lived out as a response to His summons and service."[1]

The Lord's call on Noah's life included two unique assignments: First, Noah was called to be a husband and the father of three sons. This is important. Sometimes we are looking for a great mission from God, only to neglect the very first ministry He has given us, which is usually the people we live with—our families. Next, God gave Noah the historic commission to build the Ark.

There is no way we can remain unscathed by the society around us unless we walk with God daily. Those who work in full time ministry (and often those who volunteer in ministry), are the ones delivering the message, but are not always able to attend a fellowship of believers. It is vitally important that we are able to draw close to the Lord Himself, to find grace in His eyes and to be sensitized to His will.

God revealed the coming judgment upon the earth to

Noah, and He called Noah to build the Ark that would preserve the remnant of human souls from that judgment. God also revealed that there would only be eight people saved through Noah's obedience.

I am sure that it must have been difficult for Noah to grasp the significance of this call upon his life. His sons had just been born, but God spoke to him of the wives of his sons, who would be among the saved. Noah was in for a long haul, and eventually labored for 120 years in obedience to God. He watched his family grow, and he built the Ark, following God's detailed instructions—for 120 years! Can you imagine?

Sometimes we question the call of God upon our lives because of the small number of lives impacted, or the length of time it takes to complete the job. Think of Noah laboring for over a century. Did he ever wonder if he had truly heard God correctly? Or did his daily walk with Him erase his doubts?

*God calls us to Himself.* That's important to remember. The outward work is merely the extension of that call. Daily, intimate fellowship with God can help us to labor in obedience, patiently trusting God for the outcome, asking for the strength to work without questioning, doubting, or wavering.

The day came when Noah's task was complete and God instructed him and his family to board the Ark. Sometimes in retelling the story, we forget that Noah, his wife, his three sons, their wives, and all the animals—two of each kind— sat in the Ark for seven days before it began to rain (Genesis 7:10)!

For 120 years, Noah faithfully and obediently fulfilled his call. He built the Ark, warned his family about the coming judgment, followed the Lord's instructions in safely loading them onto the boat, watched God shut the door behind them— and then waited some more.

Picture the scene. The masses jeering at him from outside—while inside, Noah's family looking at him like, well, what now? *Are you crazy, Noah? I thought you said it was going to rain...why isn't it raining, Noah?*

God had a reason for the seven-day wait. Some of it is tied into biblical prophecy concerning the last days and the rapture, or the snatching away of the church (Noah's ark is an archetype of the church being spared the coming judgment). But we can be sure that whenever God asks us to wait, He has His reasons.

Remember Naaman, the great commander of his king's army (II Kings 5)? Stricken with leprosy, and accustomed to being in command, Naaman was furious when the prophet Elisha did not just wave his hand over Naaman and heal him. Instead, Elisha sent a messenger to tell him to wash in the Jordan River seven times (there's that number seven again). After a lot of questioning and sputtering about in a rage, Naaman finally obeyed, received the healing he so desperately needed, and learned a lesson about obedience and patience.

There will be many times when the very people we care for and minister to will question our call. There will be times when we question our call. We get tired! Tired of waiting for so long to see results, and intimidated by those who mock and doubt what we're doing.

Faithful servant of the Lord, "do not grow weary in doing good" (2 Thessalonians 3:13). You can be calm and secure in the call of God. Take heart from the examples in Scripture of those, like Noah, who answered God's call, and found blessing in waiting and obedience, and in turn, blessed generations to follow.

"My main ambition in life is to be on the devil's most wanted list."

Leonard Ravenhill

# WEEK TWO
## Believing the Lord Can Use You

---
### *Vision*
---

*The next day, as they went on their journey and drew near the city, Peter went up on the housetop to pray, about the sixth hour. Then he became very hungry and wanted to eat; but while they made ready, he fell into a trance and saw heaven opened and an object like a great sheet bound at the four corners, descending to him and let down to the earth. In it were all kinds of four-footed animals of the earth, wild beasts, creeping things, and birds of the air.*

*And a voice came to him, "Rise, Peter; kill and eat."*

*But Peter said, "Not so, Lord! For I have never eaten anything common or unclean."*

*And a voice spoke to him again the second time, "What God has cleansed you must not call common." This was done three times. And the object was taken up into heaven again.—**Acts 10:9-16***

What a glorious experience when God gives us a vision like Peter's!

A vision is a revelation of biblical truth, or divine wisdom working in concert with the supernatural gifts, such as a word of knowledge and the word of wisdom. To the believer, a vision is as visible as the sunrise or sunset. It can come during a time of prayer, in the midst of a workday, or even in the morning shower.

Peter's vision was divinely connected to another vision, given to the centurion Cornelius the day before (Acts 10:3-7). God was preparing these two men for a divine appointment that would radically change the world.

Dietary laws were sacred to the Jewish community. Peter must have watched in disbelief as the Lord displayed every kind of "unclean" animal before him and told him, "Peter, kill and eat." We see Peter arguing with the Lord – even in the midst of this powerful vision! That's how hard it was for him to break with tradition. Finally, he yielded himself to God and understood. The world has changed. The door to salvation and a relationship with God had been opened to Gentiles! In

*Believing the Lord Can Use You* 5

those days, that was a very radical concept.

God in His sovereignty will accomplish His will through yielded servants. What we learn from this text is that Peter observed his vision carefully, recognized it as from God, and then, the next few verses tell us, he "wondered within himself what this vision which he had seen meant," and "while he thought about the vision the Spirit said to him..." He took the time to ponder over what he had seen and heard, to learn what God was saying

Leaders need to have vision. In *Spiritual Leadership,* Oswald Sanders wrote: "A vision without a task makes a visionary, a task without a vision is drudgery, a vision with a task makes a missionary."[2] Vision coupled with a mission changes the world. The vision God gave Peter was a graphic illustration of a spiritual truth—that God shows no partiality. The application of that truth would come in a matter of 24 hours when Peter brought the Gospel to the Gentiles in Cornelius' house—a very bold act. Peter understood now that the forgiveness of sins is for all who receive Jesus. This principle is so simple—yet so profound.

In your ministry, are you asking God for vision? You must also prepare your heart to obey that heavenly vision and to apply its message. God does not reveal a vision to us merely for the sake of information, or to make us super-spiritual. He has a purpose in mind. The Holy Spirit made it clear to Cornelius and Peter what was to be done immediately, although neither of them totally understood what the final result of their actions would accomplish. They were simply obedient to what God told them through the vision.

We have a tendency to want to speculate about what God is doing, and to help the Lord accomplish what we presume to be His plan. Peter and Cornelius, however, were simply obedient to the Spirit, and to what was communicated in the vision. It all came together in Caesarea when the Gentiles received the Gospel and were baptized with the Holy Spirit—the fulfillment of a divine vision and appointment that changed the world.

Do you believe that God can do that with you? Prepare yourself to receive a message from the Lord that will equip and inspire you to reach your community, school, or neighborhood. Set aside some time for prayer and seeking the Lord for heavenly vision coupled with a task. Set your heart on obedience, so that without hesitation you will act upon what the Lord shows you today.

# WEEK THREE
## A Valuable Lesson in Spiritual Labor

### Faithfulness of God

*But I want you to know, brethren, that the things which happened to me have actually turned out for the furtherance of the gospel, so that it has become evident to the whole palace guard, and to all the rest, that my chains are in Christ...—**Philippians 1:12-13***

Paul never ceases to amaze me. He was in prison, chained to a prison guard, waiting to find out if he will be executed by Caesar. Yet he still managed to write a letter to the Philippian church, filled with thankfulness and praise! Paul had great affection for the Philippians. "I thank God upon every remembrance of you," he wrote (Philippians 1:3). He also expressed a sincere confidence that God was doing a special work in this body of believers.

But soon, his focus shifted to the fact that he is writing from prison. The road to prison was filled with hardship, danger, and rejection. Yet, the attitude of this man is steadfast, immovable. All that happened to him—persecution, flogging, prison, fearing for his life, distress—"turned out for the furtherance of the gospel." Paul never wasted time lamenting his situation, position, or condition. "My chains are in Christ," he wrote (Philippians 1:13).

Paul had learned the most valuable lesson possible in the realm of spiritual labor: *the Lord is faithful.* We can count on the faithfulness of God twenty-four hours a day, seven days a week. I am amazed at how quickly I pray for deliverance, or lament my problems, questioning the faithfulness of the God who called me. Then God reminds me through His Word, or another believer, or a circumstance, of His unfailing love.

In the area of evangelical work today, we see a lot of writing, multiple forms of double-speak, speakers looking for ways to make everything sound positive for fear of discouraging their followers. But that is not honest! Life is hard at times. There are trials and tribulations. The focus is not on how to avoid these things, but how we can see God's faithfulness.

Paul was not that type of spiritual leader. "Who shall separate us from the love of Christ?" he asked. "Shall tribulation, or distress, or persecution, or famine, or nakedness, or peril, or sword?...Yet in all these things we are more than conquerors. For I am persuaded that neither death nor life, nor angels nor principalities nor powers, nor things present nor things to come, nor height nor depth, nor any other created thing, shall be able to separate us from the love of God which is in Christ Jesus our Lord" (Romans 8: 35-39).

Paul was a man fully persuaded that the faithfulness of God can transform any experience into the furtherance of the Gospel. He was so in love with the Lord that nothing could shake his confidence in God's faithfulness.

While the faithfulness of God is stated very clearly in Scripture, we need to experience it firsthand to be as persuaded as Paul. A servant of God heads into the storms of life and the maelstrom of ministry led by the Holy Spirit, but the enemy will try to throw us off course with fear and uncertainty. In the midst of the trials and difficulties, the faithfulness of God acts like a gyrocompass to provide a strong and steady course.

You might be going through a difficulty now that makes you feel like you are going to perish! Remember how afraid the disciples were when they crossed the Sea of Galilee, with huge waves and strong, tempestuous winds tossing the boat like a toy? They turned to Jesus, peacefully sleeping in the stern of the boat, on a pillow.

"Teacher," they cried, "do You care that we are perishing?" (Mark 4:35-41).

Like wise, we ask the Lord, *Do You care? Are You concerned about our ministry and the people we love?* And we get the same answer He gave the disciples. Jesus simply awoke, rebuked the wind, turned to the sea and said, "Peace, be still!" —and "there was a great calm."

Then He turned to His disciples and asked, " Why are you so fearful? How is it that you have no faith?"

I don't believe Jesus was accusing or scolding. He reminded His disciples that He can be trusted. Jesus personifies the faithfulness of God, at total peace in the midst of the storm. He will navigate us through the storms, and steady us with His love and faithfulness. He will finish the work He has destined for you to complete, and you can be assured that whatever happens to you—rejections, disappointments, or even chains—can be for the furtherance of the Gospel.

*O Lord, may the Spirit of God work within us to bring us to that place of fully comprehending the faithfulness of God.*

# WEEK FOUR
## Blood, Sweat, and Hot Metal

### *Perseverance*

*For they all were trying to make us afraid, saying, "Their hands will be weakened in the work, and it will not be done. "Now therefore, O God, strengthen my hands. —Nehemiah 6:9*

*"O God, strengthen my hands."*

A simple direct prayer from a man facing serious obstacles. The children of Israel were finally allowed to return to Jerusalem after 70 years of captivity in Babylon. Nehemiah, cupbearer to the king of Persia, was granted permission to help his people. After successfully rebuilding an important wall, Nehemiah soon discovered enemies among the people, conspiring to weaken and discourage him through fear and intimidation. Nehemiah resolutely stood up to the opposition. He was not about to give up, but he knew he needed help, so he called out to God to strengthen his hands.

In our modern, technologically advanced world, everything is supposed to happen instantly at the click of mouse and we except things to get done NOW. We seem to have lost the heart and will to persevere through a longer task filled with difficulties or a work that just can't easily be completed in a short time. Perseverance—the ability to stick to something until it is done—is vital to the Christian worker. The early pioneers of our land called this *"gumption."*

In Peter's letter to believers, he encourages believers to diligently grow in their faith, and exhorts us to add to our faith, perseverance (2 Peter 1:5-8). Perseverance is a trait of spiritual maturity, and helps us to bear fruit as we grow in our knowledge of the Lord. Success in any endeavor relies upon a few important things: the Lord's will, His timing, and certainly His provision. What can we bring to the work? It is usually not talent, knowledge, or riches that brings success, but perseverance that helps us finish the race. Nehemiah may have possessed other resources, but above all, he had perseverance. When the obstacles he faced seemed difficult and even dangerous, he displayed a tremendous amount of courage and perseverance by calling out to God for the strength to carry on.

*Blood, Sweat, and Hot Metal* 9

There is a distinct difference between godly perseverance and human stubbornness. Human stubbornness is self-willed (I want what I want!), whereas godly perseverance is submitted to God's will (Your will be done). A consecrated, fixed focus upon what the Lord has called you to do, allowing nothing to deter you from the task, requires the same intensity and effort as fighting for your own desires— but you receive a much greater prize, wrote Paul: "I press toward the goal for the prize of the upward call of God in Christ Jesus" (Philippians 3:14).

Nehemiah's mission was to rebuild the walls of Jerusalem. God had placed a vision with a specific task before him, and he was not going to allow the enemy to use fear to distract him. The enemy will use personal attack, ridicule, threats, physical exhaustion, and fear of failure to pull you away from the ministry. But you can persevere, because it is God's will for you to fulfill His purposes.

When I think of the word *perseverance*, I picture a blacksmith heating up a piece of metal. It begins to glow red hot in the forge. The blacksmith beats upon the red hot metal to give it a thin edge and a sharp point. Then he plunges it into a barrel of water to temper it. The tempering allows the metal to harden and hold its sharpened edge. Likewise, the process of tribulation forges godly determination and perseverance in your soul, giving you the strength to press through and keep your edge.

Nehemiah prayed continually for God to strengthen his hands. The focus of his prayers was always on the Lord and His ability to empower him for the work. His view of God was always greater than his perception of the enemy. Remember that as you serve the Lord. You can press on through the difficulties because the Lord will strengthen your hands for the work.

# WEEK FIVE
## In Whom Do I Believe?

### Reality of God

*God, who at various times and in various ways spoke in time past to the fathers by the prophets, has in these last days spoken to us by His Son, whom He has appointed heir of all things, through whom also He made the worlds; who being the brightness of His glory and the express image of His person, and upholding all things by the word of His power, when He had by Himself purged our sins, sat down at the right hand of the Majesty on high, having become so much better than the angels, as He has by inheritance obtained a more excellent name than they.*
**—Hebrews 1:1-4**

Isn't it amazing that we can serve the living God and at times totally forget that He is real? This statement sounds ridiculous but I know it is true.

The Lord spoke through the prophet Isaiah to the children of Israel about this very matter: "You have forgotten the God of your salvation..." (Isaiah 17:10-11). Isaiah says it is possible to forget the God who saves us, the Lord who provides for us. We can get caught up in the activities of ministry, go through the motions of ministry, and lose sight of the reality of God.

In this text of Hebrews we see that in these last days God has revealed Himself to us through His Son. Jesus Christ is the brightness of His glory, the expressed image of His person. The person of Jesus Christ is being made tangible through the person and work of the Holy Spirit.

There are times in ministry that are extremely difficult. The issues of disease, death, and senseless violence bring pressures upon our hearts and minds that are hard to bear. It is not that we doubt the existence of God, but in the midst of so much sorrow and hardship, we can lose the *reality* of God.

We can all too easily find ourselves acknowledging a historical savior, a deity that exists in principle but not on a practical, personal level—even though He has proven Himself on those levels! The children of Israel observed God's power in dramatic ways again and again during their deliverance from

*In Whom Do I Believe* 11

Egypt. His provision for them, His protection of them, His encouragement through Moses and Aaron, and their ultimate freedom from Pharaoh were miraculous evidences of God's power and presence. The first thing they forgot when things got hard was the supernatural presence of God. They forgot, "the Lord will fight for you...He is my strength and my song" (Exodus 4:14,15:2) and looked for human leadership instead.

As we read these familiar stories in the Bible, we wonder how could the children of Israel possibly forget God or doubt the reality of God when He was so obvious?

We are capable of the same spiritual blindness. There is no greater demonstration of God's power than a transformed life. To have our sins purged and our hearts opened to the Word of God is a miracle we forget. Paul the apostle proclaimed in his second letter to Timothy, "...for I know whom I have believed and am persuaded that He is able to keep what I have committed to Him until that Day" (2 Timothy 1:12). Paul *knows* the One he trusts. God is not just a vague deity. He is someone Paul personally knows.

Our faith is a personal expression of belief in the person of Jesus Christ. We are not simply following an ideology or creed, but the person of Jesus, Himself. It is this reality that we must hold onto daily in the ministry. God, who in the past, at various times, in various ways, spoke to the fathers by the prophets, has in these last days spoken to us by His Son, the text declares. We have the Holy Spirit dwelling within us (1 Corinthians 3:16), and the Word of God ever before us and in us as well. We are given the greatest resources in all of creation!

It is vitally important that we refresh ourselves daily with the reality of God; only then can we be effective in our ministries. Don't let yourself fall into the trap of the routine or of just meeting a social need. When we lose the reality of God our first response is to return to Egypt. When we lose the reality of God we look for human leadership and soon we find ourselves in bondage again.

Pray today that your eyes will see the Son and all that He has done in you and for you. May the Lord become real to you again and your service inspired by Him.

# WEEK SIX
## Ask for Everything

### Answers to Prayer

*"It shall come to pass in that day that I will answer,"
says the Lord; "I will answer the heavens, and they
shall answer the earth. The earth shall answer with
grain, with new wine, And with oil; They shall answer
Jezreel. Then I will sow her for Myself in the earth,
And I will have mercy on her who had not obtained
mercy; then I will say to those who were not My
people, 'You are My people!' And they shall say, 'You
are my God!' "* **—Hosea 2:21-23**

One of the most encouraging books I've ever read is
*Answers to Prayer* by George Muller,[3] a simple journal of the
many answered prayers during Muller's ministry to orphans in
nineteenth century England. He started three orphanages,
which he oversaw on faith, meaning that Muller never revealed
their needs to anyone or asked publicly for help. He simply
prayed for everything. Workers, buildings, food, furniture,
everything was lifted up to the Lord in believing prayer. His
prayer journal is exciting to read because he recorded everything that God answered in those forty plus years, including
the hardships and times of testing, and how God proved His
faithfulness again and again.

In this text from Hosea, God made a powerful promise to
remove the reproach from Israel and betroth her to Himself, in
righteousness, justice, lovingkindness, and mercy. The Lord
also promised abundant blessings and provision—grain, new
wine, and oil—as well as love and mercy. The stigma of rejection or of being outside of God's people was removed, as the
Lord declared, "I will say to those who were not My people, 'You
are My people!' And they shall say, 'You are my God!'" What a
wonderful promise from the God of the universe! The God who
cannot lie, and who will not forsake!

God promises to answer as we lift up our many needs to
Him. There is nothing too small, nothing too big. George
Muller prayed for a single penny as well as for thousands of
British pounds. Millions of dollars flowed through George's
hands in the course of his ministry, to help the poor and

*Ask for Everything* 13

needy. He had successfully learned the first basic principle of ministry: God answers prayer.

My wife and I planted a church in the rural community of Ramona, California in November of 1984. It was a total venture of faith; we started with absolutely nothing. We had no money in the bank, and not even a job, as I left my staff position at another church to start the new church. The church body prayed for us and sent us out with their blessing. We had two sons, ages five and one. I was convinced that God was leading us and learned my own awesome lessons in how God answers prayer.

We simply, prayerfully proceeded in the ministry, asking the Lord for everything, every step of the way. He provided a rented elementary school multi-purpose room and two class-rooms for services. He provided for our basic needs for four months until I got a job. He provided the people who began to attend the weekly services. I worked full time for an electronics company and served as pastor of the new church for a year. Then the Lord allowed me to leave the electronics job in February of 1986 to pastor the church full time. God was and is faithful to answer prayer! Eight years after planting the church we turned it over to the assistant pastor, Rob Hubbard. I took a position as Administrative Pastor for Calvary Chapel of Escondido. Pastor Rob Hubbard is presently faithfully caring for the flock in Ramona. The church has grown to over 900 people and continues to be a blessing in the community.

There are times when we can falter, and wonder if God will truly answer our prayers. We will experience trials that test our faith, as well as times when we simply need to wait upon the Lord. But always, ultimately, we can take God at His Word, because He promises to answer. We are betrothed to Him forever.

# WEEK SEVEN
## Exercising Godliness

### *Finishing Well*

*If you instruct the brethren in these things, you will be a good minister of Jesus Christ, nourished in the words of faith and of the good doctrine which you have carefully followed. But reject profane and old wives' fables, and exercise yourself toward godliness. For bodily exercise profits a little, but godliness is profitable for all things, having promise of the life that now is and of that which is to come. This is a faithful saying and worthy of all acceptance. For to this end we both labor and suffer reproach, because we trust in the living God, who is the Savior of all men, especially of those who believe. These things command and teach. —1 Timothy 4:6-11*

The apostle Paul wrote to young Timothy out of concern for him. He offered him some good advice, encouraging him to be "nourished in the words of faith and of the good doctrine which you have carefully followed." Doing this, he says, will make him a "good minister," and help him finish well.

To be a good minister of Jesus Christ is to finish well. Paul did not fear rejection, injury, or even death for himself or his young disciple. What weighed heavily on his heart was the quality and purity of their teaching. He did not ever want to be disqualified as a good minister due to lack of sound doctrine or being swayed by "profane and old wives' fables."

Timothy was a young man when he met Paul. Raised by a believing mother and grandmother, Timothy's natural father was Greek. Paul became a spiritual father to Timothy, instructing him in spiritual matters. A special bond developed between them, as they endured many hard times, and rejoiced together in the victories of ministry.

I once served in the military and went to war with other young men. I have traveled with committed men and women on short-term mission trips to several countries. A tremendous bond is forged between those serving side by side on the battlefield. It runs deeper than a casual friendship, but rather becomes a very personal, lifelong relationship. As a pastor,

*Exercising Godliness* 15

one of my greatest joys is seeing someone I've discipled enter into fruitful service in the Lord. One of my greatest heartbreaks is to see someone fall and go back to the world. It's not hard to understand the bond between Paul and Timothy, and Paul's concerns for his young friend's spiritual well-being.

"Exercise yourself toward godliness" Paul exhorts Timothy. With fitness centers almost on every corner, exercise is a popular activity in our culture. Men and women in America spend a lot of money on "bodily exercise" and all the accessories that go along with it—which Paul points out "profits little" because it only affects one person. No matter how fit you become, it primarily benefits you. Is exercise wrong? Of course not. It's good to take care of yourself. But our priority needs to be "godly exercise." What if we, as a culture, directed that same time, money, effort, and concentration on spiritual things? Just think how it would impact the world! Paul's exhortation to Timothy is timeless and applies to us as well. The profits of godliness affect our lives now, and "that which is to come" (4:8).

Paul had an incredible command of language. He was free born, a Roman citizen, raised in a Greek culture. As a Jew of the tribe of Benjamin, Paul was a Pharisee of great intellect and influence. But not until he came to know Jesus Christ, did he attain true wisdom. By his own testimony, he declared that everything he knew before knowing Jesus was "rubbish" (Philippians 3:8). He threw out all his credentials but one: the qualification he described in verse ten: *"...because we trust in the living God, who is the savior of all men, especially of those who believe."* He follows this with the simple exhortation, *"These things command and teach."*

Paul wisely reproduced himself through disciples like Timothy. And, he knew what was important in life. He determined for himself, and taught those he loved, the importance and joy of finishing well.

Dear fellow servant, I pray that you will know the joy of finishing, of running the race to the end. I have yet to see anyone fall away and end up happy and content.

Keep it simple, stay on course, please "don't grow weary while doing good" and follow Paul's simple exhortation. It is not our education or our experience that really matters, but it is our apprehension of these simple truths that will enable us to *finish well.*

# WEEK EIGHT
## *Are You Talking to Me?*

---

### *Call of God, Moses*

*Now Moses was tending the flock of Jethro his father-in-law, the priest of Midian. And he led the flock to the back of the desert, and came to Horeb, the mountain of God. And the Angel of the Lord appeared to him in a flame of fire from the midst of a bush. So he looked, and behold, the bush was burning with fire, but the bush was not consumed. Then Moses said, "I will now turn aside and see this great sight, why the bush does not burn." So when the Lord saw that he turned aside to look, God called to him from the midst of the bush and said, "Moses, Moses!" And he said, "Here I am." Then He said, "Do not draw near this place. Take your sandals off your feet, for the place where you stand is holy ground." Moreover He said, "I am the God of your father—the God of Abraham, the God of Isaac, and the God of Jacob." And Moses hid his face, for he was afraid to look upon God. — Exodus 3:1-6*

What strikes me about the call of God on the life of Moses is the timing and means.

Because the children of Israel were in bondage in Egypt, they cried out to the Lord. He heard their groanings, saw their suffering, and honored His covenant with Abraham, Isaac, and Jacob by providing a deliverer in the person of Moses.

Moses had been tending his father-in-law's flock of sheep in the Midian desert, where he had been living for 40 years after running from his own problems in Egypt. He married Zipporah who bore him a son, Gershom, whose name means stranger, because, Moses said, "I have been a stranger in a foreign land."

Moses had finally grown content as a shepherd and family man in the deserts of Midian. No longer the proud man of Pharaoh's court who had hastily fled from his crime of passion, he had become a simpler man, emptied of self, pride, and conceit. It took just a few days for Moses to leave Egypt, but it took 40 years for the influence of Egypt to leave Moses.

The king of Egypt died, God heard the cries of His people,

and Moses was finally ready to answer God's call upon his life.

The sight of a burning bush that was not being consumed by flames must have been a curious spectacle. Drawn to the bush more by curiosity than any spiritual compulsion, Moses heard the Lord call his name.

Have you ever heard the Lord call you by name? It is a powerful and intimate experience. Look at the response of Mary Magdalene in the Garden of Gethsemane by the empty tomb, when Jesus called to her, "Mary!" She recognized His voice immediately, even though she couldn't recognize him physically. She thought He was the gardener until He spoke—and then she knew right away it was Jesus and ran to embrace Him; she thought she had lost Him once, and couldn't bear to lose Him again. We can see the devotion and close relationship between Mary and her Lord in this encounter.

In the back of the desert, Moses was stunned when he heard the Lord call his name, but his response was an immediate, "Here I am." After the Lord warned him not to draw too near, and to remove his sandals, "for the place where you stand is holy ground," Moses hid his face, afraid to look upon the most holy God, out of reverential fear. Then Moses began his dialogue with the Lord as God laid out the call and the plan: "I will send you to Pharaoh that you may bring My people, the children of Israel, out of Egypt."

To which Moses immediately replied, "Who am I that I should go to Pharaoh, and that I should bring the children of Israel out of Egypt?"

I can relate. The Lord placed the call upon my life during a Sunday evening service. I was a young Christian, eagerly listening to my pastor, Mike MacIntosh. I sat in the back of the church, a mass of people in front of me, and all I saw was hundreds of nameless heads of various colors, shapes, and sizes—a sea of black, brown, red, balding, long hair, short hair; countless, nameless heads.

Then the Lord spoke to me, softly and firmly. "Richard, I want you to feed my sheep." I responded, like Moses, "Lord, who am I? I don't know anything. I'm still a young Christian."

The Lord simply said again, "Richard, I want you to feed my sheep." I quietly responded, "OK, Lord, I will do whatever you want." At that moment all the nameless heads became people with faces, names, needs, and questions. Every day from that day forward, everything I did was in preparation for the day the Lord would place me in full time ministry. The day

18    *Press On: 52 Reasons to Stay in the Race*

came four years later in a similar manner, as the Lord again spoke in that still, small voice.

Be looking for the "burning bush" in your life, and listen for that firm, loving voice of our God, calling you to serve Him. Don't shrink back because of your inadequacies; trust that God will supply all that you need to serve Him. He will say to you what He said to Moses and to every servant who answers His call: "I will certainly be with you" (Exodus 3:2).

"A revival is nothing else than a new beginning of obedience to God."

Charles Finney

# WEEK NINE
## Reflection of God's Face

### *Vision*

*"And it shall come to pass afterward that I will pour out My Spirit on all flesh; your sons and your daughters shall prophesy, your old men shall dream dreams, your young men shall see visions. And also on My menservants and on My maidservants I will pour out My Spirit in those days."*
**— Joel 2:28-29**

Imagine the Day of Pentecost. A mighty wind rushes through the house. Tongues of fire light up the disciples' countenances, as the Holy Spirit falls upon them. Peter stands before the crowd, speaking words, through the gift of prophecy, once proclaimed by the prophet Joel.

The Lord promised, first through Joel, then Peter, to "pour out My Spirit on all flesh," empowering the believer by the "*epi*" or "upon" experience of the Holy Spirit. Joel gave voice to God's promise that "your sons and your daughters shall prophesy, your old men shall dream dreams, your young men shall see visions." Everything about the entire second chapter of Joel urges us forward toward restoration, renewal, and a revived, intimate relationship to God.

I find it interesting that the old men will dream the dreams, but the young men will see visions! I was young when the Lord called me into the ministry and now, over 25 years later, I am older, but God is still giving me visions. Apparently I don't qualify as an old man yet. When the dreams begin to replace the visions I suppose that will indicate my crossing over to old age. The young men are to be alert, awake, watching for the things of God. The Lord will speak to them through visions, providing direction and revelation. Peter, Paul, and John all witnessed glorious visions after Pentecost. We cannot be effective in ministry without being enabled by the Holy Spirit. The baptism of the Holy Spirit transforms the believer into a vessel for fruitful ministry.

I desire for the Lord to grant me vision to plant new churches, just as Paul was led to Macedonia through a vision. I even more strongly desire to have the kind of relationship

*Reflection of God's Face* 21

with the Lord Moses experienced. Read Numbers 12:6-8 and see what a marvelous encounter Moses had with the God of the universe! God tells him that He will speak to prophets in visions and dreams, but to Moses He speaks face to face, "plainly and not with dark sayings." Moses spoke with God as a friend, and even saw His "form," which is interpreted as being a "reflection" of God or manifestation of Christ. Scripture says that no man has seen God at any time (John 1:18), but that Jesus is the visible image of the invisible God (Colossians 1:15).

Have you ever seen the back of your head? Have you really observed it directly? No! You have only seen it by looking in a mirror. You have only seen the *reflection* of your head in the polished glass. Moses visibly saw the reflection of God's face, and visually witnessed the trailing edge of His glory. Paul the apostle received his revelation directly from Jesus in the deserts of Arabia (Galatians 1:12). Abraham had lunch with Jesus Christ by the terebinth trees in Mamre (Genesis 18:1-33).

With the indwelling and the baptism of the Holy Spirit, we too can have waking visions and an intimate relationship with God. The prophecy was given in Joel, and fulfilled in Acts 2:14-25. We are the young and old men spoken about in the text. We can have the revelation and vision our ministry desperately needs.

I encourage you to pray for the kind of fresh, waking vision that will transform your walk with Jesus Christ. Look at Peter. From the carnal, unspiritual man he was before Pentecost, he became the humble man of vision we meet after Pentecost. God took a flawed, imperfect man and used him in mighty ways.

May all who serve the Lord be filled with the Holy Spirit, and may we be given glorious vision to inspire and encourage us to press on!

# WEEK TEN
## When Common Sense Doesn't Matter

### *Faithfulness of God*

*And Elijah the Tishbite, of the inhabitants of Gilead, said to Ahab, "As the Lord God of Israel lives, before whom I stand, there shall not be dew nor rain these years, except at my word." Then the word of the Lord came to him, saying, "Get away from here and turn eastward, and hide by the Brook Cherith, which flows into the Jordan. And it will be that you shall drink from the brook, and I have commanded the ravens to feed you there." So he went and did according to the word of the Lord, for he went and stayed by the Brook Cherith, which flows into the Jordan. The ravens brought him bread and meat in the morning, and bread and meat in the evening; and he drank from the brook. And it happened after a while that the brook dried up, because there had been no rain in the land.*
**—1 Kings 17:1-7**

Few of us have a ministry as dramatic as Elijah's, although I know there are times when we wish we could be a mighty man of God like Elijah, calling fire down from heaven, praying for and witnessing miraculous healing, seeing the mighty hosts of heaven.

How can we minister with this same dynamic power and confidence in God? Is there a process or method we can follow to experience such a powerful ministry?

Elijah had no program or secret method for success. The strength of his ministry was his relationship with God. Early on, he learned to rely upon God's faithfulness. He called upon God's faithfulness to do the impossible. He survived by the faithfulness of God's provision, protection, and guidance. As servants of a mighty God, we must cling to the faithfulness of God at all times: in the quiet that precedes the fierce spiritual battles; in the heat of the battle when we are weary or scared; in the aftermath, when we are often left to minister to the wounded. Oh, how we need to understand and believe in God's faithfulness to survive the battles!

One of the first times in Scripture we meet Elijah, the

Tishbite of Gilead, he is prophesying to the wicked King of Israel, Ahab, that a severe drought is imminent, and will last three and a half years. The Lord directed Elijah, through a word of knowledge, "Get away from here ... and hide by the Brook Cherith, ... you shall drink from the brook, and I have commanded the ravens to feed you there." The Lord provided for Elijah, with drink, food, and a safe place to hide. The Brook Cherith was an obscure little stream of water where no one would think to look for a prophet. We don't know the exact location of the brook then or now, but it most likely was east of the Jordan River in Samaria.

As Elijah obeyed the Lord and stayed by the brook, God faithfully sustained him, while the rest of the land suffered through the drought.

So often we doubt and fear when difficulties come! We wonder how we will survive when there is no visible way of provision. The drought is over the entire land. How can we be fed when there are no crops in the fields or animals in the stall? And then God used the most unlikely of all creatures to bring Elijah bread and meat in the morning and evening— an unclean bird. The raven is an infamous thief, a predator that feasts on dead things, and a bird specifically described as needing help finding its own food (see Job 38:41). Only God would think of such a means of provision to glorify Himself and to teach the prophet to trust and obey.

And then the Brook Cherith dried up, and it was time for Elijah to move on. God had even greater plans for him, and if you follow the rest of the story in 1 Kings, you will see how God continued to provide for Elijah along the way.

I was pastoring a church once during a time when the men of the congregation were largely unemployed. The United States was at war in the Persian Gulf and the economy had taken a hit. The offerings fell to less then half of what they normally had been. We had enough to pay the church bills but not enough to pay the pastor. My wife and I prayed and the Lord instructed us to sell our home. The real estate market was at a standstill. Nothing was selling, and if it did, not for the asking price. We continued to pray and pressed forward. God provided a cash buyer who offered above our asking price and for almost twice what we paid for the house four years earlier!

That's when God gave me these Scriptures about Elijah. The money He provided for us sustained us for two years, until the ministry recovered. It was the Lord's provision through the ravens. The economy doesn't matter to the Lord, common sense doesn't matter to the Lord, because He is Lord of all! He opens doors that cannot be opened by anyone else. I am so thankful for the faithfulness of God!

"The only way to learn strong faith is to endure great trials."

*George Muller*

# WEEK ELEVEN
## *The Making of the Valiant*

---
### *Perseverance*
---

*These are the names of the mighty men whom David had: Josheb-Basshebeth the Tachmonite, chief among the captains. He was called Adino the Eznite, because he had killed eight hundred men at one time.*

*And after him was Eleazar the son of Dodo, the Ahohite, one of the three mighty men with David when they defied the Philistines who were gathered there for battle, and the men of Israel had retreated. He arose and attacked the Philistines until his hand was weary, and his hand stuck to the sword. The Lord brought about a great victory that day; and the people returned after him only to plunder.*

*And after him was Shammah the son of Agee the Hararite. The Philistines had gathered together into a troop where there was a piece of ground full of lentils. Then the people fled from the Philistines. But he stationed himself in the middle of the field, defended it, and killed the Philistines. And the Lord brought about a great victory. Then three of the thirty chief men went down at harvest time and came to David at the cave of Adullam. And the troop of Philistines encamped in the Valley of Rephaim.—2 Samuel 23:8-13*

The victories of three of King David's men are recorded in these passages of Scripture, for all generations to read. They are described as "David's mighty men," and were known as soldiers, experienced in battle. But they were not always mighty warriors. They came to David as social outcasts (1 Samuel 22:2). Under David's leadership they found a purpose for their lives, and matured into mighty, valiant warriors who would follow their captain anywhere.

David faced Goliath, the nine-foot champion of the Philistines, when the Philistines and Amalekites were the common enemy of the children of Israel. David's courage became legendary, but what truly made him a great military leader and later king, was his faith and confidence in the Lord, which gave him the strength to persevere in the face of dangerous enemies and circumstances. David's example gave the men he led the same confidence and ability to persevere and become his mighty warriors.

Josheb-Basshebeth, the Tachmonite, was the chief among the three captains. He was also called Adino, the Eznite, because he killed eight hundred men at one time.

Eleazar, the son of Dodo the Ahohite, earned his reputation by standing in defiance against the Philistines, even after the rest of the men of Israel retreated! When all the men of Israel ran away from the battle, Eleazar ran *into* the battle. "He arose and attacked the Philistines until his hand was weary, and his hand stuck to the sword." What a picture of perseverance! A man of faith, his hand resolutely gripping his sword, heading into battle, even if it meant going alone! He fought until the Lord brought victory that day. Although he grew weary, he never let go of his sword.

When we grow weary in the midst of daily spiritual battles, the key to victory is **perseverance**, with our hand firmly stuck to the sword. The Word of God is the instrument from which we draw our strength to fight, as our faith and confidence are renewed daily by the refreshing Spirit of the Living God.

Shammah, the son of Agee the Hararite is the third great leader, and he defended a crucial bean field. When the Philistines banded together in a troop, Israel's men fled, except for Shammah, who stationed himself in the middle of the lentil field. The term "troop" is a description of a crowd or camp of men. There is no specific number mentioned but we know that Shammah was greatly outnumbered. He was determined to fight to the death, defending the field, and the Lord gave him a great victory that day.

Each of these three courageous men is an example to us of how we can be transformed by the Lord from men in distress and debt to mighty men of God. David's example of consistent faith, courage, and perseverance in the battle, inspired these men to achieve beyond their own talents and skills, because they learned faith, courage and perseverance.

Perseverance is defined as standing firm in the face of difficulty and pressing through. Even when we see little or no progress or immediate fruit, we press through, firmly planted, our hand stuck to the sword, our eyes riveted on our King, our Captain, Jesus Christ, until the enemy is routed.

It can take twenty years to impact a community with the Gospel. When a ministry is planted and begins to lay a solid foundation of teaching the Word, touching the community with the love of Christ, tearing down strongholds in prayer, and bringing the lost to faith, God will honor the perseverance of those who serve. As the people begin to live out their faith, year by year, the church will become a vital part of that community, influencing the schools, businesses, and government.

In the early 1980s, our church sent Bibles to all graduating seniors of the local high school[4]. We started a crisis pregnancy center that in over 20 years has saved over a thousand babies' lives[5]. A fruitful ministry takes time and perseverance to touch a community.

May we press on against overwhelming odds, despite the size of our enemy—or even if no one stands with us. Remember, God stands with us and the victory is His!

Serve Him until He comes again.

*The Making of the Valiant* 29

"Without Christ, not one step; with Him, anywhere!"

David Livingstone

# WEEK TWELVE
## Simple Yet Profound

### *Reality of God*

*"And without controversy great is the mystery of godliness: God was manifested in the flesh, justified in the Spirit, seen by angels, preached among the Gentiles, believed on in the world, received up in glory."*
**—I Timothy 3:16**

The Scriptures contain many great mysteries, but perhaps "the mystery of godliness" is the most profound. The word mystery is translated from the Greek word, mysterion, which is different from our normal usage. We define mystery as something unknown, or knowledge withheld. The scriptural usage means truth revealed. In the Greek culture, "mysteries" were religious rites and ceremonies practiced by secret societies into which one could be received, once they were initiated into the society's secrets. Initiates possessed certain knowledge that was not imparted to the uninitiated. The apostle Paul, writing to his young friend Timothy, implied that there are some things known only to those who are a part of the body of Christ, and who, by the Holy Spirit, can understand the revelation of spiritual truth.

In Colossians, Paul talks about " the mystery which has been hidden from ages and from generations, but now has been revealed to His saints." Mysteries in Scripture are "made known," "revealed," or "manifested" (see Colossians 1:26-27), and the truths revealed always show us the reality of God.

Paul wrote to Timothy concerning this great "mystery of godliness" as he described the required characteristics of those in church leadership, which includes the ability to keep hold of "the mystery of the faith with a pure conscience" (1 Timothy 3:9). Ministers of God must possess the capacity to understand the deep truths of the faith, and we must have faith in a living God— the God who created the universe, revealed Himself in human life, submitted to death on a cross, rose from the dead, and redeemed mankind, before ascending to heaven.

Let's look at how Paul defined the "mystery of godliness,' as he breaks down this "great truth revealed," and at other

*Simple Yet Profound* 31

areas of Scripture where these truths are confirmed:

"God being manifested in the flesh" — "And the Word became flesh and dwelt among us..." (John 1: 14-18).

"...justified in the Spirit"— "When He had been baptized, Jesus came up immediately from the water; and behold, the heavens were opened to Him, and He saw the Spirit of God descending like a dove and alighting upon Him" (Matthew 3:16). The Spirit affirms the Messiah in fulfillment of prophecy.

"...seen by angels"— throughout Scripture angels acknowledge Jesus as Lord. Angels proclaimed His birth, helped save His life from Herod, strengthened Him in the Garden of Gethsemane, and were at His Resurrection. They continually reveal His glory continually to all of creation, and in the end, they marvel that such a mighty God is so mindful of man (Psalm 8:4).

"...preached among the Gentiles..." —One historic day the Apostle Paul declared, "Therefore let it be known to you that the salvation of God has been sent to the Gentiles, and they will hear it!" (Acts 28:28). The Word of the Lord continued to be preached to those outside the Jewish faith, and, for the first time, through the Holy Spirit, Gentiles began to believe in the one true God. Sinners were made aware by the Spirit of their lost conditions, and began to cry out for forgiveness—and that work has continued on throughout history, as Jesus continues to save the lost. The message of the Gospel is a Person, not a precept. As Chuck Missler stated on a recent radio message, "Christ did not come to make bad men good. He came to make dead men alive, and lost men found."

"...believed on in the world..."—Jesus talked to His heavenly Father in the Garden of Gethsemane, as He prayed for those He came to save: "I have manifested Your name to the men whom You have given Me out of the world" (John 17:5-8). Then Jesus prayed for you and me specifically, "I do not pray for these alone, but also for those who will believe in Me through their word..." (John 17:20). We have come to believe in Him through their eyewitness testimony. Finally, John sums up the purpose for our ministries in John 20:31: "...but these are written that you may believe that Jesus is the Christ, the Son of God, and that believing you may have life in His name."

"...received up in glory." —Jesus rose from the dead, and ascended to the right hand of the Father, making intercession for us. As Stephen, the first martyr of the church, was dying, he cried out, "Look! I see the heavens opened and the Son of Man standing at the right hand of God!" (Acts 7:56). For him, the reality of God was confirmed, as it has been for thousands of other believers throughout the ages. There is definite, absolute, evidence to believe in the reality of God. (Read also Hebrews 8:1 and Colossians 3:1.)

We have the same adversary Jesus faced in the wilderness after 40 days of fasting. Satan's tactics against Jesus are the same tactics he uses against us. He challenged Jesus' deity, he challenged God's provision, and he challenged God's protection. He challenges the reality of God in our personal walk of faith. If he can get us to believe in a mere historical Jesus, or an ideological Christ, then he has found a foothold for undermining our faith.

As a believer, you have been given the Holy Spirit as a Teacher and Comforter, and He will reveal to you the great truths of God's Kingdom. Get a firm grip upon this great mystery, and may you allow God to hold you firmly in His grip.

*Simple Yet Profound*

"If you as ministers of Christ are not very prayerful, you are to be pitied."

*Charles Spurgeon*

# WEEK THIRTEEN
## *Eternal Perspective*

### *Answers to Prayer*

*A Psalm of David.*

*Hear my prayer, O Lord, give ear to my supplications! In Your faithfulness answer me, and in Your righteousness. Do not enter into judgment with Your servant, For in Your sight no one living is righteous. For the enemy has persecuted my soul; He has crushed my life to the ground; He has made me dwell in darkness, Like those who have long been dead. Therefore my spirit is overwhelmed within me; My heart within me is distressed.*

*I remember the days of old; I meditate on all Your works; I muse on the work of Your hands. I spread out my hands to You; My soul longs for You like a thirsty land. Selah. Answer me speedily, O Lord; My spirit fails! Do not hide Your face from me, Lest I be like those who go down into the pit. Cause me to hear Your lovingkindness in the morning, For in You do I trust; Cause me to know the way in which I should walk, For I lift up my soul to You.*

*Deliver me, O Lord, from my enemies; In You I take shelter. Teach me to do Your will, For You are my God; Your Spirit is good. Lead me in the land of uprightness. Revive me, O Lord, for Your name's sake! For Your righteousness' sake bring my soul out of trouble. In Your mercy cut off my enemies, and destroy all those who afflict my soul; for I am Your servant.*
**—Psalm 143**

I love the honesty of David. You don't have to wonder how David was feeling at any particular time. He was not ashamed to put it all out there; he was honest with God about his thoughts, feelings, and spiritual condition. David's intimacy with the Lord, the way he talked to God, honestly and personally, and the manner in which he wrote the Psalms reflect a consistent, dynamic prayer life. I've learned that

*Eternal Perspective* 35

I need to invest time in my relationship with the Lord, or I won't experience that same intimacy and freedom of expression that David had.

Prayer is a dialogue, not just a monologue. As David pours out his heart, he allows opportunity for the Lord to respond. You can tell that David expects an answer. In the opening of Psalm 143, David pleads for God to listen to his "supplications," then requests, "InYour faithfulness answer me." David knew that answered prayer would not come through his own faithfulness, but in the faithfulness of God.

In verses two through four, David writes of the enemy who persecutes and crushes his soul, casting him into the darkness of the dead. He feels completely overwhelmed, and distressed in his heart. Can you relate? Do you ever feel so crushed and full of despair under the relentless assaults of the enemy, that you too are overwhelmed? It is indeed a spiritual battle, and there are moments in each of our lives, when we feel like we just cannot go another step.

But then something wonderful happens as the Holy Spirit jogs our memory. Right around verse five, David begins to turn around. He remembers the "days of old" as he meditates on all that God has done in his life, and reflects upon the glory of His creation. His sights are raised to once again see the eternal perspective. When we focus on the temporal perspective, our hearts are overwhelmed. We cannot deal with the trials or the fear. But as we spread our hands out in simple surrender, our souls long for Him like a thirsty land, and we know that because of God's faithfulness, that thirst will be quenched, and our hearts comforted.

Answers to prayer come in three simple responses: Yes. No. Wait.

David asked for a speedy answer. He pretty much told the Lord, *"Hurry up, before I completely lose it! Please don't hide from me...don't let me fall! Please let me hear Your words of love in the morning!"*

Most of the time when we pray, if we are honest, we are looking for a "yes" answer. We have our own predetermined plan for deliverance or provision, and we would just like God to make it happen. But David's prayer, as desperate as it sounds, was also a surrender to God's will. After pleading for help, he stated, "I have put my trust in You." Then immediately, after abandoning himself to God's care, he asked the Lord to show him "the way in which I should walk. For

I lift my soul to You."

What a beautiful example of devotional prayer. David was not being superficial here, but sincerely asked the Lord to cause him to experientially know where he should go and how he should do it. David took shelter in the Lord, and settled all doubt when he declared in verse ten, "You are my God."

When we pray, we need to expect God to answer, and be willing to submit ourselves to His sovereign will, trusting in His faithfulness, acknowledging His righteousness, hiding ourselves in His presence. We must be able to say, "I trust in You. You are my God."

There are circumstances in my life right now that are just too big. People who seem impossible to reach, needs greater than I can meet. It can be overwhelming. But then I remember the faithfulness of the Lord. I meditate on all of God's works. I pray, like David finished this psalm, *"Revive me Lord, destroy my enemies, and give me the strength to stand. For I am your servant!"*

And I long to hear the Lord's voice and find assurance in His presence. I desire to bury my head into His chest and hear Him say it is going to be all right. For then I will know that God's response is sufficient. He is my God.

"Beware of reasoning about God's Word – obey it."

Oswald Chambers

# WEEK FOURTEEN
## Addicted to Ministry

---
### *Finishing Well*
---

*Watch, stand fast in the faith, be brave, be strong. Let all that you do be done with love. I urge you, brethren—you know the household of Stephanas, that it is the firstfruits of Achaia, and that they have devoted [addicted] themselves to the ministry of the saints*
**— 1 Corinthians 16:13-15**

Paul had a burden to help believers finish well. He wanted the church to stay strong, united and faithful. So he closed his first letter to the Corinthians with five exhortations to the church, which are certainly as apt today as they were in the first century. He wrote with military terminology, as if addressing the Lord's soldiers.

1. **Watch**— This is  term describes a sentry on duty; be vigilant, attentive, believers, Paul wrote, on the look-out for the enemy. Our enemy is real and will attempt to infiltrate our ranks to destroy us from within.  An outright frontal attack would be obvious and we would surely use all of our spiritual defenses.  However if we become complacent, lazy, or let our guards down, he can sneak in and destroy us from within. We need to watch for the enemy, and stand guard for each other.

2. **Stand fast in the faith** — With our feet firmly planted, and our hearts submitted to Christ, we need to make a conscious decision to stand fast.  In the Roman military, men in battle never broke ranks.  Training is the same today, to stand fast in the battle. Five times in the New Testament and twice in the Old Testament we are taught how essential it is to stand fast, resolved, and immoveable in our faith. That's why it is important to know what we believe and why we believe it.

3. **Be brave**—This term appears only once in the New Testament and 24 times in the Old Testament, and is translated, "act like a man."  Because we have the Spirit of God, we need not be fearful, timid, or cowardly.  Living the Christian life requires the courage to resist when others are bowing to ungodly social norms.  We are not to be ashamed of the Gospel.  Bravery is not the absence of fear, but moving forward

*Addicted to Ministry*  39

and overcoming the fear. Paul understood that.

Read 2 Corinthians 7:4-6, and you will see how Paul, beset by fears, recognized the Lord's comfort and encouragement.

4. **Be strong** —We can be strong, firm, steadfast in the Lord, " in the power of His might" (Ephesians 6:10)—because the Lord is faithful to exchange our weakness for His strength. Like a father who assists his son in a task too big for him, carrying most of the actual weight, our heavenly Father gives us the strength to follow His will and serve His people.

5. **Let all that you do be done in love** —Oh that we could make this happen! Imagine every action and attitude governed with love. This verse is *all* inclusive; all means the whole deal, *everything*, is to be done with *Agape* love; giving to others without thinking of ourselves.

Finally, in verse 15 we meet the household of Stephanas, the first converts in the church in Achaia (Greece)—and they are addicted to the ministry of the saints! "Addicted" may seem like an odd term, and some translations use the word "devoted." But the point is, this family had a very powerful commitment and testimony. An addiction governs the lives of the addicts, and these believers' pursued that addiction daily, like a craving, ministering to the saints.

Would anyone say of us that we have addicted ourselves to the ministry of the saints? Oh that we would desire to serve the Lord with such a passion!

# WEEK FIFTEEN
## *"I Will"*

---

### *Call of God, Abraham*

---

*Now the Lord had said to Abram: "Get out of your country, from your family and from your father's house, to a land that I will show you. I will make you a great nation; I will bless you and make your name great; and you shall be a blessing. I will bless those who bless you, and I will curse him who curses you; and in you all the families of the earth shall be blessed." So Abram departed as the Lord had spoken to him, and Lot went with him. And Abram was seventy-five years old when he departed from Haran.*
**—Genesis 12:1-4**

Get out of your country. Walk away from your relatives, the comfort and security of your family home; surrender everything familiar and dear, and go – even though you're 75 years old. And trust in God for direction and a purpose.

Wow! Few of us will ever receive such a call upon our lives. It is amazing, really, that Abram (later called Abraham) accepted this call so readily. We don't know if he struggled or if his wife, Sara, protested being uprooted, but we do know that God spoke to him and made unconditional promises of blessings—and Abraham believed Him and obeyed.

The Lord made five "I will" statements, which set the foundation for Abraham's journey:

**"I will [show you a land]...I will make you a great nation...I will bless you and make your name great...I will bless those who bless you...I will curse him who curses you."**

Then the Lord dropped a bombshell: "And in you all the families of the earth shall be blessed." This is no small event between a man and his Lord—especially when the man and his wife are technically beyond the child bearing years! The scope of this call is historical, monumental, beyond the ordinary. Later, we read in chapter 17, the Lord even changed Abram's name to Abraham. Abram is "exalted father," but Abraham means

*"I Will"* 41

"father of a multitude." His new name even proclaims this dramatic call upon his life!

In modern times, there are a few well known believers who have been called by God, like Abraham, to lives that have left an indelible mark upon our nation and the world. Millions of people have been touched by the simple obedience of a humble preacher named Billy Graham. Pastor Chuck Smith is another man who answered a call that changed millions of lives through Calvary Chapel. I have had the privilege to meet and hear these men, and am always touched by their humility and obedience. Abraham, Billy, and Chuck would agree unanimously that they did not, and could not, have fully comprehended the scope of God's call upon their lives. They simply embraced it in faith and committed to being obedient. I know they would also agree that there are thousands of lesser-known believers, faithfully answering the call upon their lives, serving people and changing the world in ways we cannot always see.

The key to fruitful ministry is obedience to the call of God, without trying to figure out exactly how God is going to do what He promised. If we concentrate first on being obedient each day, as well as patient and consistent with the tasks set before us, we can stand back in awe as we watch God develop the ministry just as He said.

Our confidence needs to be in God, and not in our own ability or stamina. Abraham was 75 years old when God called him, but the Lord didn't make His covenant with Abraham for 24 years. In those 24 years God worked in his life, preparing Abram to become Abraham, the father of many nations.

Are you wrestling with the call of God upon your life right now? Are you complaining that the Lord is taking too long to do what He promised? We can learn many lessons from Abraham. He experienced lapses of faith where he tried to force the promises prematurely (Hagar and Ishmael), and he had times of great faith, when he trusted in God's promises, even to the point of being willing to give up his only son, Isaac.

How can we learn to live and minister with such trust, embracing the things of God? "So Abram departed as the Lord had spoken to him," we read at the end of our Scripture. Abraham did not negotiate, reason, speculate, or procrastinate. He began the journey with confidence in the Lord who called him. We can do the same, giving up all our worries about timing and circumstances, knowing that God is faithful and will fulfill His promises.

Abraham left the familiar to embrace the unknown. He trusted his God, period. May we learn how to let go and live for Him—and answer His call.

*"Obedience to the call of Christ nearly always costs everything to two people – the one who is called, and the one who loves that one."*

Oswald Chambers

# WEEK SIXTEEN
## *Lord, They Don't Understand*

---
### *Vision*
---

*And when we had finished our voyage from Tyre, we came to Ptolemais, greeted the brethren, and stayed with them one day. On the next day we who were Paul's companions departed and came to Caesarea, and entered the house of Philip the evangelist, who was one of the seven, and stayed with him.*

*Now this man had four virgin daughters who prophesied. And as we stayed many days, a certain prophet named Agabus came down from Judea. When he had come to us, he took Paul's belt, bound his own hands and feet, and said, "Thus says the Holy Spirit, 'So shall the Jews at Jerusalem bind the man who owns this belt, and deliver him into the hands of the Gentiles.'"*

*Now when we heard these things, both we and those from that place pleaded with him not to go up to Jerusalem. Then Paul answered, "What do you mean by weeping and breaking my heart? For I am ready not only to be bound, but also to die at Jerusalem for the name of the Lord Jesus." So when he would not be persuaded, we ceased, saying, "The will of the Lord be done." And after those days we packed and went up to Jerusalem.* — **Acts 21:7-15**

When God gives us a vision for ministry, three things are inevitable.

1. We must be obedient to the vision.
2. There will be spiritual opposition.
3. There will be times when you are the only one who understands the vision.

After Paul's third missionary journey, God gave him a vision to return to Jerusalem. Paul wanted to be sure he was there for the feast of Pentecost (Acts 20:16). In his farewell address to the Ephesian elders, he explains, "I go bound in the spirit to Jerusalem, not knowing the things that will happen to me there, except that the Holy Spirit

*Lord, They Don't Understand* 45

testifies in every city that chains and tribulations await me." Paul focused on being obedient to the vision, and never considered shrinking back from the consequences, even though he clearly knew he was in for hard times.

Such obedience and clarity of purpose are the keys to true spiritual power in the life of the believer, given by the Holy Spirit. That is the power that enabled Jesus Christ to go to the cross. It is the power that drove Paul to follow the Spirit's leading, no matter where it took him.

The Holy Spirit can be very clear in directing the believer to a specific place, and in revealing what awaits that person. A vision based upon the gifts of wisdom, prophecy, and word of knowledge will bring about exhortation, comfort, and edification to believers. Paul was not swayed by the well-meaning concerns of his brothers and sisters. Not even Agabus' dramatic prophecy deterred him. Paul is completely compelled by the vision God gave him to go to Jerusalem.

Spiritual opposition can take many forms. One is a direct attack by our enemy, Satan, another is through our own fears. But perhaps the most difficult is the opposition from well-meaning family members, or other Christians. A direct attack by the devil is hard, but at least you can respond with spiritual weapons at a recognized enemy. Satan is usually predictable. He attacks us with the same strategy he used in the Garden with Eve, and in the wilderness against Jesus. He will question God's Word, and he will try to plant doubt in your heart about God's protection, provision, and sovereignty. We can fight the fear this may cause by encouraging ourselves in the Lord, and fortifying ourselves with the Word.

The most difficult spiritual opposition, however, is what we encounter from our own family and spiritual leaders. Every place Paul went, his brothers and sisters in the Lord tried to convince him to stay away from Jerusalem. Out of genuine concern they tried to override the vision God had given Paul. What they said may have made sense on a human, practical level, but Paul knew what God had told him. We just aren't always capable of discerning the purposes and plans of God, which is why we need to be led by and obedient to the Holy Spirit. We need to hold onto the vision God has given us, pressing forward, even if no one else understands! The fulfillment of the vision will come in due time, and then others will have the opportunity to glorify God.

Grab a hold of verse fourteen and make it yours: *"The will of the Lord be done."*

"Christian, remember the goodness of God in the frost of adversity."

Charles Spurgeon

# WEEK SEVENTEEN
## Help Me With My Unbelief

### Faithfulness of God

*If we are faithless, He remains faithful; He cannot deny Himself." — 2 Timothy 2:13*

We can absolutely rely upon the faithfulness of God. It is our own concept of Him that fails us. In our finite minds, we often think of God as a supernatural entity detached from His creation, rather than the personal heavenly Father whose thoughts for us are more numerous than the grains of sand on the seashore. This personal Deity desires fellowship on a daily basis—with us. He is a Father who loves us with compassion, and inhabits our praises. He is our God and He is faithful, even when we are faithless.

I have found that sometimes it takes a determined act of our wills to remember who God is, because we are so easily affected by our circumstances. We are exhorted in sermons and studies to not live for this world, to keep a light touch because we are not of this world. But daily we are besieged with responsibilities, obligations, and the difficulties of daily living, so we get discouraged and tired. I've often thought that the paperwork alone it takes to live these days, plus the responsibility of bills, trying to do business with answering machines, and forging our way through traffic are all annoying, fiery darts, designed to test our patience and rob our joy. Then when the heavy trials come, and we are spiritually weak, instead of counting it all joy, we fall into the depths of self-pity and wonder where God is and if He is real.

The children of Israel were not allowed into the Promised Land for 40 years because of their unbelief! But the Lord still took care of them, and ultimately fulfilled His promises. In spite of their faithlessness, God remained faithful to them.

Jesus and His disciples were sailing across the Sea of Galilee, which is eight miles across at the widest point, when a huge storm arose (Mark 4: 35-41). While Jesus calmly slept in the stern of the boat on a pillow, they were being tossed about by giant waves. I've seen those waves! We were in Israel in March of 1992 when a sudden a storm hit that generated waves over nine feet on the Sea of Galilee. The town of Tiberias was flooded[6]. So I can understand why the disciples were afraid and thought they were going to drown. They woke Jesus up and practically accused Him of neglecting them: "Teacher, do you not care that we are perishing?"

Jesus' response was to get up, rebuke the storm, and still the sea. Then He turned to the disciples and asked, "Why are you so fearful? How is it that you have no faith?" Jesus was able to sleep during the storm because He had absolute assurance of getting to the other side.

There are times when we think that God is not concerned or perhaps even unaware of our situation, and we falter and wrestle with our lack of faith. But God is greater than us and it is He that keeps us. He wants us to look to Him and not our circumstances. He remains faithful.

This is not an excuse to become complacent or lazy in our walk with Christ. It is an encouragement to press onward and endure. Throughout this chapter of 2 Timothy Paul reminds us to be diligent, to be strong "in the grace that is in Christ Jesus," and to "endure hardship," so that we can "approved to God." "Approved" means to be tried and found to have passed the test.

But none of this is possible in our own strength, and I find that reassuring, because I would fail everyday without the faithfulness of God. The Lord is faithful to keep His promises, and to help us with our unbelief. He will transform us into men and women with a living, vibrant faith in the personal God of our salvation.

You might be doubting the faithfulness of God today, as you labor under hardship, overwhelmed, sure you are perishing. I pray that you will believe and know that God is faithful even when we are faithless. He will demonstrate His love and faithfulness to you, I am certain of it. Press through, and immerse yourself in His Word until you hear that still, small voice answer your questioning heart. He remains faithful, for He cannot deny Himself.

# WEEK EIGHTEEN
## The Blessings of Old Age

---
### *Perseverance*
---

*Then the children of Judah came to Joshua in Gilgal. And Caleb the son of Jephunneh the Kenizzite said to him: "You know the word which the Lord said to Moses the man of God concerning you and me in Kadesh Barnea. I was forty years old when Moses the servant of the Lord sent me from Kadesh Barnea to spy out the land, and I brought back word to him as it was in my heart. Nevertheless my brethren who went up with me made the heart of the people melt, but I wholly followed the Lord my God.*

*So Moses swore on that day, saying, 'Surely the land where your foot has trodden shall be your inheritance and your children's forever, because you have wholly followed the Lord my God.' And now, behold, the Lord has kept me alive, as He said, these forty-five years, ever since the Lord spoke this word to Moses while Israel wandered in the wilderness; and now, here I am this day, eighty-five years old. As yet I am as strong this day as on the day that Moses sent me; just as my strength was then, so now is my strength for war, both for going out and for coming in. Now therefore, give me this mountain of which the Lord spoke in that day; for you heard in that day how the Anakim were there, and that the cities were great and fortified. It may be that the Lord will be with me, and I shall be able to drive them out as the Lord said."*
**—Joshua 14:6-12**

Imagine bragging at the age of 85 that you feel as strong as you did in your forties! We should all be so blessed, as Caleb was, a man of spiritual maturity and physical strength who persevered well into his old age.

Joshua and Caleb were close friends and allies as they served the Lord together. As part of the team of twelve spies Moses sent in to spy out the Promised Land, they saw the beauty and fruitfulness of the land. They also saw giants but were unafraid. They believed they could defeat the giants and take the land, because God was leading them. The other ten spies, however, came back with a negative report, completely

*The Blessings of Old Age* 51

forgetting the Lord as they reacted to fear and doubt. Their unbelief basically amounted to a refusal to enter the Promised Land, and caused the Israelites to wander for 40 years in the wilderness. An entire generation perished in the wilderness, except for Joshua and Caleb.

These men could have split off from the rest of the tribes. They could have stiffened their necks, and led a rebellion into the Promised Land because they believed God was with them. But instead they submitted themselves to God's hand, through the leadership of Moses, and served Moses and the people, as they looked toward the day that they would enter this beautiful promise from God.

Caleb was a man of faith and perseverance. In our text we hear Caleb recounting the events of that day 45 years ago, when he was 40 years old and sent to spy out the land. He brought word back to Moses of what was in his heart—the excitement and promise of a new land! But the other ten spies caused the heart of the people to melt in fear and dismay. Then he added the simple statement. "...but I wholly followed the Lord my God." The act of obedience to the Lord, even though we might be convinced of a spiritual truth, is a test of spiritual character.

Caleb had the ability to press on, day after day, in patient expectation and confidence in the God who was leading him. I believe that is at least part of what gave him the strength and vitality he enjoyed in his old age. A man of 85 as fit and strong as he was at 40! His reward, when he finally arrived in Canaan, was to inherit the mountain of Hebron, full of trees to clear, and giants to dispatch. Caleb ultimately succeeded and was blessed.

That is the reward of perseverance. When serving the Lord there will be situations in which we believe we should press forward, knowing we are spiritually justified, but the Lord says no. We are to wait, or allow another ministry to move into that area. Our human wisdom, logic, and pride might affect our decision making because we feel like we're going to lose out, or miss the promise of God. But, like Caleb, we need to submit our plans and hopes to the Lord, even if it takes years to see the fruit of our obedience.

Remember, it is not talent, skill, a charismatic personality, or an education that will win in the end. These things alone will not bring a fruitful ministry or spiritual success. Perseverance will prevail. It is the faithful plodders who submit to the Word of the Lord, and to the leadership God has put over them. "Remember those who rule over you, who have spoken the word of God to you, whose faith follow, considering the outcome of their conduct," Hebrews 13:7 reminds us. We are given leaders we can emulate and confidently follow because God put them there. Our generation is impatient and quick to follow our own way. Let us slow down and seek the Lord and be willing to spend 40 years in the wilderness if that's what it takes to come into the fullness of His promise. Charles Spurgeon once said, "By perseverance the snail reached the ark."

May we press toward the city whose maker and builder is God, staying true to what is in our hearts, but willing to persevere.

*"Prayer is not a monologue, but a dialogue. God's voice in response to mine is its most essential part."*

*Andrew Murray*

# WEEK NINETEEN
## Learning to Let Go

---
### *Reality of God*
---

*For thus says the Lord, Who created the heavens, Who is God, Who formed the earth and made it, Who has established it, Who did not create it in vain, Who formed it to be inhabited: "I am the Lord, and there is no other. Tell and bring forth your case; yes, let them take counsel together. Who has declared this from ancient time? Who has told it from that time? Have not I, the Lord? And there is no other God besides Me, a just God and a Savior; There is none besides Me.*
**—Isaiah 45:18, 21**

We can be so busy with ministry related activities that we actually forget the wonderful truth that God is real. Overwhelmed with the huge needs of the people, we can begin to think it is our responsibility to save them. Everyone I know in Christian ministry has felt this burden at one time or another.

When I was a new Christian, zealous to share my faith and lead people to Jesus, I became discouraged when new believers didn't change their lifestyle right away. I was reading a book on discipleship published by the Navigators, and I came upon a quote that I have never forgotten. "Jesus has called us to become fishers of men. However, Jesus says, 'You catch them, I will clean them.'"

There is only one Savior, one God, one Lord, and we are not Him. All of Isaiah chapter 45 is a wonderful affirmation of God as Creator, and Savior, especially when he declares in verse 22: "Look at Me and be saved, all you ends of the earth! For I am God and there is no other." He is the only true God.

Now, in my rational mind, I don't believe I have a God complex, nor do I consider myself divine. But there are times when I'm guilty of taking the weight of the ministry upon my shoulders. I'm sure this is true for you as well. We can become so consumed with people's problems that we agonize over how to solve them. A few years ago, driving home after a difficult counseling session, I was burdened with the problems of the couple I had been counseling. Their problems seemed beyond

*Learning to Let Go* 55

help, and I felt like a failure and a spiritual lightweight. The enemy was right there to condemn and to point to my own human inabilities. Then the Lord showed me something very profound. I looked down at my hand on the steering wheel and noticed a scratch, a recent wound from working in the yard. The Lord spoke to me, "Richard, do you see that scratch? The best you can do is clean it with soap and water, maybe a little antiseptic, and bind it with a bandage. You clean it and bind it...only I can heal it."

In an instant my burden lifted, the condemnation left me, and the enemy was forced to retreat! God reminded me that He is God, and there is no other God beside Him. He is responsible for mankind. He is responsible for the ministry, and only He can change hearts. My responsibility was obedience, to clean and bind, and trust Him to do the rest.

I've seen too many men and women leave the ministry burdened and overwhelmed, feeling like failures. Without realizing it, they had subtly shifted their faith in the Lord to trusting in their own abilities, knowledge, or even anointing. Even Jesus did not heal every sick or troubled person around Him. He chose only twelve people as His closest friends. He did not go in person to meet the needs of every individual in the world. Yet, at the end of His life He prayed, "I have finished the work which You have given Me to do" (John 17:4). He trusted in His heavenly Father, that if He completed His mission, God the Father would make sure everything important was accomplished —and indeed it was.

Jesus knew, while He walked this earth, that God is real. Being able to *know*, to firmly grasp the reality of God is what will set us free. God is not an icon, a legend, a philosophy, or a disinterested supreme being. He is not a piece of wood carved into an image to which we pay homage. He is not just a force or a faceless power to fear or pacify. He is a personal, living God, the only true God. He is the compassionate, loving, faithful, righteous, all-powerful, tenderhearted God of our salvation. And He is real.

Take a reality check today of your life and ministry Where are you today? Have you placed the Lord in a place of intellectual sovereignty and not in practical reality?

Our lives can be like a pizza. We divide it into slices, compartmentalizing it into sections: our work, our family, our ministry, our hobbies, our friends, etc. Sometimes we even make the slices thinner, to cram more things in our lives. And then we make the terrible mistake of letting God become just one of the slices in our life. Sometimes He is the slice that gets cut even thinner, or left out all together.

In reality, God is the whole pie, and our lives are meant to be filled with Him. That's when everything fits, and our lives and ministries flourish. God is real and on the throne! Rejoice!

"Talking to men for God is a great thing, but talking to God for men is greater still."

E.M. Bounds

# WEEK TWENTY
## Lord, I Need to Hear From You

### *Answers to Prayer*

*The Lord has sworn by His right hand and by the arm of His strength: "Surely I will no longer give your grain As food for your enemies; and the sons of the foreigner shall not drink your new wine, for which you have labored. But those who have gathered it shall eat it, and praise the Lord; those who have brought it together shall drink it in My holy courts." Go through, go through the gates! Prepare the way for the people; build up, build up the highway! Take out the stones, Lift up a banner for the peoples!* **—Isaiah 62:8-10**

In July of 1989 I had the opportunity to go with a team into China to bring Christian materials to a pastor of an underground church in Guangzhou. A month earlier, in June 1989, the government had put down a short-lived revolution for democracy. Student led demonstrations led to violence in Beijing, and many were killed. The western press was banned, and Americans were advised not to travel to China. We were rerouted from Beijing to Hong Kong. Our Chinese contacts in Hong Kong would only agree to lead us to Guangzhou if we truly believed the Lord wanted us to go. I needed to hear from the Lord! I needed a specific answer to prayer. If we were arrested in China at this time, it could mean detention for an indefinite amount of time—or worse. All the platitudes I'd casually uttered over the years—"I'll pray about it" or "let's seek the Lord"— suddenly   seemed trite and shallow.

I had taught for many years that God answers prayer. I've read many of the numerous books written on the subject of answered prayer. I knew that the Bible tells us that if we pray according to the will of God, He hears us, and in hearing us He will answer us (1 John 5:14-15).

I truly believed then and now that God always answers prayer. He will say *yes, no,* or *wait*—but He always answers. That day in China, when I had a serious decision to make, I found myself thinking of the believers in Acts 12:15. They had prayed and asked the Lord to deliver Peter from prison. But when God miraculously delivered Peter, and Peter walked up,

*Lord I Need to Hear From You*  59

knocked on the door of the house where they were gathered to prayer, they simply didn't believe it! They tried to tell the girl answering the door that she was crazy. In fact, they left Peter standing outside, still knocking, while they argued about it. When they finally did open the door, and saw Peter standing there, they were shocked!

This text is very significant to me, because God used it to change my life. That day in China, I was in my room, praying and begging the Lord to answer my prayers so clearly that there would be no mistakes. If we were going to continue on this mission, I needed to know, specifically, that it was God's will for us to smuggle Christian materials in to Pastor Samuel Lamb's underground church.

God brought me face to face with His power and incredible answered prayer. During my daily reading I came to the above passage in Isaiah, and through it, the Lord spoke so clearly to me that it almost seemed audible. He told me we would bring the materials in safely, and enjoy fellowship with these grateful believers. "Go through, go through the Gates!" He said.

My heart leaped for joy in the message of Isaiah, but also the manner in which God answered my prayer. My life changed that day. I grew more confident in the Word of God, in the assurance of answered prayer, and desired to change the way I lived. I wanted a deeper faith.

Seven of us, two women and five men, traveled by train to Guangzhou and delivered the materials to Pastor Lamb. I was able to speak to Pastor Lamb and ask him questions about leading people to a closer walk with Jesus. Pastor Lamb had endured 20 years in a prison labor camp connecting train coal cars. His faith remained strong, he told me, because he had memorized so much of Paul's pastoral epistles. He experienced the reality of answered prayer in the depths of that Chinese prison.

I will never forget that trip and the words of these Scriptures are very dear to my heart. Pursue God and pray believing. Let your actions match your theology. Listen with your heart and read the Word with your eyes, and you will hear Him speak those wonderful answers you eagerly seek.

God answers prayer!

# WEEK TWENTY-ONE
## Crossing the Finish Line

### *Finishing Well*

*We are bound to thank God always for you, brethren, as it is fitting, because your faith grows exceedingly, and the love of every one of you all abounds toward each other, so that we ourselves boast of you among the churches of God for your patience and faith in all your persecutions and tribulations that you endure...*
**—2 Thessalonians 1:3-4**

As you work hard in your ministry, does it ever begin to feel like an endurance contest? And you are just hoping you can make it to the finish line?

Crossing the finish line of a twenty-six mile marathon leaves runners dripping with perspiration and physically spent. When people retire at the end of a long career, they also often look physically spent, aged, and exhausted, and are ready for a life of leisure.

In the life of the Spirit, however, we don't really "retire" but we do run the race. My prayer for you—and for me as well—is that finishing will be a lot different than collapsing across a finish line or heading for a permanent vacation.

The apostle Paul was excited about what he saw in the Thessalonians. First, he noted that their faith was growing "exceedingly" and impacting their community and nation. They were experiencing an active, living, growing faith. They were like marathon runners who, after the first twenty-six miles, were still refreshed and ready to keep going.

It is my prayer that your faith is growing and maturing every day. A growing faith keeps us strong and energized. In the early years of ministry, sometimes we are fueled by zeal and excited enough to take great steps of faith. As the years go by, it's easy to fall into an ordinary routine and become complacent, even cynical and jaded. Our steps of faith become smaller and smaller, as our hearts grow cold. It's tragic, really—but it doesn't have to happen this way! Older does not mean spiritually tired or less enthusiastic. We *can* finish well. That was certainly one of Paul's strongest desires. He thanked

*Crossing the Finish Line* 61

God for the testimony of the Thessalonians, as an encouragement to him and to the rest of the Church.

Continuing to exercise our faith will keep us young and strong. Remember Caleb (See WEEK EIGHTEEN, *The Blessings of Old Age*)? He was 40 years old when Moses sent him to spy out the Promised Land. He didn't actually get to occupy this dreamed of land until he was 85! What if he had shrugged his shoulders and said, *"Hey, I'm ready to retire. I'm old. It's too late for me. I'm tired."*

Instead, we read that he had the strength and vigor of a 40-year-old man (Joshua 14:7-13)! Caleb had the strength for war and for conquering the land. I know he might have been blessed with extraordinarily good health, but I believe part of what gave him this strength and vitality was his willingness to continue on with the Lord, to take those steps of faith. Caleb was the picture of "finishing well."

Next, Paul commended the Thessalonians for their "abounding" love for one another. What a beautiful fellowship; a body of believers with an exceedingly growing faith and love for one another. This is a church I would like to attend! This is a ministry that we can hope to emulate and glorify God.

But in spite of their energy and deeds of love, their lives were not easy or always fun. This was a fellowship that also suffered great persecution and hardship, which I'm sure is partly what drew them together and kept their hearts soft toward the Lord. We know that difficulties and trials bring people together, and drive us to our knees as God becomes more real. The horrific events of September 11, 2001 in New York, Washington D.C., and a field in Pennsylvania prove this. Those with an active, living faith reached out in love to the wounded and dying. Many sacrificed themselves for the sake of others on that day. Our entire nation was changed. Churches were filled, and people cherished their families and lives in a new way. But in a few years, since that awful day, many hearts have grown cold and complacent once again.

I pray that we will be challenged by the Thessalonians to live dynamically, and that our lives will be inspired by a faith that never stops growing, stretching, maturing, and taking us to new places with the Lord. I pray that we will learn to love one another abundantly, even in the midst of our hardships and trials. May our desire to "finish well" cause us to press forward in great steps of faith no matter how long we have been laboring in the field. May we all finish well!

# WEEK TWENTY-TWO
## Courage Under Fire

### Call of God, Gideon

*Now the Angel of the Lord came and sat under the tere-binth tree which was in Ophrah, which belonged to Joash the Abiezrite, while his son Gideon threshed wheat in the winepress, in order to hide it from the Midianites. and the Angel of the Lord appeared to him, and said to him, "The Lord is with you, you mighty man of valor!"*

*Gideon said to Him, "O my lord, if the Lord is with us, why then has all this happened to us? And where are all His miracles which our fathers told us about, saying, 'Did not the Lord bring us up from Egypt?' But now the Lord has forsaken us and delivered us into the hands of the Midianites." Then the Lord turned to him and said, "Go in this might of yours, and you shall save Israel from the hand of the Midianites. Have I not sent you?" — **Judges 6:11-14***

There are times when the Lord calls us to do something that is literally impossible. Something so beyond our resources, capabilities, and strength, that we know it has to be His call, and His doing, or it just isn't going to happen.

When we look upon a community, or a county or even an entire country that needs to be reached with the Gospel, it can seem impossible. When we are faced with planting a church in hostile territory, we can feel overwhelmed. When we are up against a task so daunting and scary, that it looks completely out of reach, we are afraid. But then the Lord speaks to us in that still, small voice, "I am with you... go in this might of yours...have I not sent you?"

Gideon was hiding out in the winepress, threshing wheat, fearful of his enemies, the Midianites. Gideon was not famous or rich. He was the least in his tribe, and his tribe was the smallest of all the tribes. He also wasn't very courageous. And yet, to this insignificant, rather spiritually weak man, an angel of the Lord appeared, and called him "a mighty man of valor."

"The Lord is with you," the angel said. But Gideon had a hard time believing it. He was in a very bleak place spiritually, and more inclined to argue than accept the fact that God could be calling him to a mighty deed. "If the Lord is with us, why has all this happened?" he complained. If we're in a similar state of mind when God calls, then we'll be just as incredulous as Gideon and find ourselves thinking, *why would God want to use such an unspiritual, fearful individual as me?*

"The Lord is with you," that angel said —and that makes all the difference in the world. The presence of the Lord is what transforms scared, insecure people into men and women of valor.

In the military soldiers are given medals for actions above and beyond the call of duty. The Distinguished Service Cross and the Medal of Honor are the two highest medals given for valor in battle against an enemy force. They are awarded to those who risked their lives in extraordinary ways, setting them apart from their contemporaries. Most of the time, the Medal of Honor is awarded posthumously; most soldiers make the ultimate sacrifice in earning such an award. In 1944 the Valor device was authorized as an attachment to the Bronze Star Medal. The Valor device is awarded in recognition of a valorous act (the "V") performed during direct combat with an enemy force. It may also denote an accomplishment of a heroic nature in direct support of operations against an enemy force, in a non-combat role.

All these medals are awarded to soldiers who have fought and demonstrated courage under enemy fire.

Gideon was described by the Angel of the Lord as a man full of courage under fire, a man of valor— before he even actually fought the Midianites! The Lord sees us through His eyes, and transforms us into the minister He wants us to become. We are called, equipped, and sent out in the might of almighty God. What a wonderful relief it is to understand this truth. When God calls us to the ministry, He provides the courage to face the enemy, and to experience victory through His mighty power.

We can be encouraged by the characters we meet throughout the Bible. Over and over, we see how God called regular, flawed people to accomplish impossible deeds and glorify His name. That means he can use me —and you! I am actually a candidate to be a man of valor, even though I am sometimes fearful and question the presence of God.

Pastor Mike MacIntosh of Horizon Christian Fellowship once told me, "Never look at your resources first, when you believe God is calling you to a specific task, because you will limit what can be done. You will never have the resources to do what God is showing you. Look to God for the vision, go forward in faith, and watch God bring the resources that will accomplish the task."[7]

I pray that you will be encouraged to answer the call of God in the course of your daily life. He will call us into battle, as He desires to plant new churches, evangelize new territories—and use us! You are a candidate for valor, even if you think you are like Gideon: afraid, insignificant, and spiritually weak. Allow God to transform you today!

"Faith expects from God what is beyond all expectation."

Andrew Murray

# WEEK TWENTY-THREE
### Responding to Spiritual Needs

---
### *Vision*
---

*And a vision appeared to Paul in the night. A man of Macedonia stood and pleaded with him, saying, "Come over to Macedonia and help us." Now after he had seen the vision, immediately we sought to go to Macedonia, concluding that the Lord had called us to preach the gospel to them.* **—Acts 16:9-10**

Paul was busy making plans to preach the Gospel in Asia, Mysia, and Bithynia, and to travel with a team into Troas, when everything changed. In the middle of the night, while everyone slept, a man appeared to Paul, pleading for help in Macedonia. Even though Paul was actively serving the Lord, actively pressing forward in what he believed to be God's will, he recognized that the vision came from God, and that the Holy Spirit was leading him in a different direction—and he didn't hesitate to follow.

God, in His sovereignty, uses visions to direct our path. Some people are called visionaries, implying that they possess a special gift that makes them more capable of receiving visions. A vision is a communication from God, through the ministry of the Holy Spirit. It is not something any of us can make happen on our own. Vision can come in the midst of actively serving in ministry, pressing for the open door, and listening for God's voice. Or, a vision can occur when we least expect it, as it did to Paul on the road to Damascus, or in the example above, when he was busy making entirely different plans. The vision is God's doing. What's important is how we respond.

Receiving a vision is not a function of our eyes, but of an open, sensitive heart—a heart that desires to be in sync with the heart of the God who saved us.

There is a fascinating biological fact about the human heart. Every cell beats, in its own unique rhythm. If you slice off a cell and look at it under the microscope, you can observe it beating. If you take a cell from a different heart, it also beats, but in a different rhythm. Amazingly, when these two cells touch, they immediately synchronize![8] They begin to beat together, in a new, harmonic rhythm. Spiritually, the same thing happens in our relationship with God. In a beautiful, miraculous way, when we are touched by God's heart, our hearts immediately synchronize with His.

Jesus' disciples were gathered together one day, trying to deal with the aftermath of the crucifixion. They were afraid of the Jews and no doubt trying to make sense of it all, when the risen Jesus appeared in their midst. "He breathed on them, and said to them, 'Receive the Holy Spirit'" (John 20:22). The original Greek text makes it very clear that Jesus acted *upon* the disciples, and they actively *received* this action. Their hearts were touched by His, and from this moment on, they began to live like disciples in sync with the Lord.

We receive what God gives. We desire vision for our ministry, but we cannot manufacture a vision through our own spiritual efforts. The vision will come as we go about serving the Lord, and when He knows we are ready to receive His revelation.

Notice that Paul *immediately* obeyed the vision he experienced, and headed for Macedonia. He didn't waste time asking why he couldn't go to Mysia, or Bithynia, or Asia, but accepted the fact that God wanted him in Macedonia.

We waste so much time speculating, grumbling, questioning God's actions and Word, when we should simply obey! Imagine how much more effective we could be if we would yield immediately when the Lord shows us His will. Imagine if the disciples doubted the vision of the risen Jesus standing before them! What if Paul had doggedly stuck to his original plans, ignoring the vision before him? But Paul focused on one thing: preaching Christ and Him crucified, wherever and whenever the Lord granted him opportunity. There was no other agenda dictating his life, and he wasted no time when the Lord spoke.

The interpretation of a vision is usually very simple, and requires a response to a spiritual need, rather than physical. Paul concluded that the Lord was calling them to bring the Gospel to Macedonia, which ultimately opened the door for the Gospel into the European continent. There was a great spiritual need in that part of the world, and it was about to be met.

In our quest for vision we need to guard against being distracted by physical need, so that we can respond to the spiritual need. We also need to guard against over spiritualizing

68   *Press On: 52 Reasons to Stay in the Race*

and analyzing the vision, and as long as we see no contradiction of Scriptures, we need to just take it literally and act accordingly. Paul didn't spend a lot of time analyzing or asking why. He just knew God had spoken and he went.

What an exciting life we can lead, and what fruit we will see in our ministries when we are obedient and when we allow our hearts to beat in rhythm with the Lord's!

Serve Him with all your heart, mind, soul, and strength, and trust Him for the vision that will guide your life.

"I have found that there are three stages in every great work of God; first, it is impossible, then difficult, then it is done."

*Hudson Taylor*

# WEEK TWENTY-FOUR
## *God Forgets My Sin But Remembers Me*

### *Faithfulness of God*

*But Zion said, "The Lord has forsaken me, and my Lord has forgotten me." "Can a woman forget her nursing child, and not have compassion on the son of her womb? Surely they may forget, yet I will not forget you. See, I have inscribed you on the palms of My hands; Your walls are continually before Me."*
**—Isaiah 49:14-16**

Have you ever felt like God has forsaken you? In the difficulties and tragedies of this life, in this fallen world, sometimes it feels as if God has forgotten us. But then we need to look into His Word and read passages like this one in Isaiah, and be reassured once again that God is faithful. That He never forgets us.

He asks the question in this passage, is it possible for a nursing mother to forget her child and its need to be fed every two hours? Most women who have given birth and know the constant demands of a young life would protest that it is impossible. But God says, "surely they may forget...." God knows that in our human state, something so intense and demanding could happen, or a woman could be so clouded by sin and selfishness, that, unbelievable as it seems, she could forget her little one.

But God says of Himself, in contrast, "Yet I will not forget you. See, I have inscribed you on the palms of My hands." This is one of the seven thousand promises of God in the Bible directed to us, His children.

Look up Jeremiah 31:34, in which God says, "...they all shall know Me, from the least of them to the greatest of them... For I will forgive their iniquity, and their sin I will remember no more." Meditate on the verse in context, and in light of what we have just discovered. Isn't it fascinating that God in His sovereignty would choose to remember **us** and to forget our **sin**? He has made it impossible to forget us because He has inscribed us on the palms of His hands.

The book of Isaiah is often called a miniature Bible. The Bible has 66 books, 39 in the Old Testament, and 27 in the

New Testament. Isaiah contains 66 chapters. The first 39 are prophecies of judgment. Chapters 40 - 66 prophesy comfort, hope and restoration when the Messiah, their Savior comes.

In these chapters, Isaiah foreshadowed the crucifixion of Jesus; especially the nail wounds that leave an imprint that will never go away. Thomas touched the wounds on Jesus' hands after the Resurrection and declared, "My Lord and my God!" The Jews will see the marks when Jesus comes again. When they ask Him about the scars on His hands, He will tell them He was wounded "in the house of my friends" (Zechariah 13:6).

Whether we are suffering through financial problems, a deep personal loss, a split in the ministry, or a crisis of faith—whatever befalls us, we cannot say that God has forgotten us. Because it is impossible. God, by His own Word, has declared that He will never forget us.

I know there are times in ministry when it seems like our prayers have no effect. In fact, sometimes it feels like the more we pray, the worse things get. When there is no fruit on the vine, no ox in the stall, when we cry out to God, "I will do anything You ask of me, just give me a word!" the silence drives us to our knees.

Barriers are erected in our spiritual life through unconfessed sin, or a hard, calloused heart. But God loves us so much that He will allow us to finally reach the unscalable wall at the end of the road, where we are incapable of helping ourselves and have nowhere else to go. The Holy Spirit reveals the barriers and asks us to allow Him to break them down.

When the children of Israel complained that the Lord was hidden from them and ignoring their needs, the prophet Isaiah responded: "Have you not heard? The everlasting God, the Lord, the Creator of the ends of the earth, neither faints nor is weary. His understanding is unsearchable. He gives power to the weak, and to those who have no might He increases strength" (Isaiah 40:27-29).

Read those words and be encouraged, as God ministers to your heart. He will give you strength to press on because He is so faithful. He is faithful to forget our sins, and to remember our human frame. We are just dust.

He is faithful to give us enough courage to get us through the storm—until the wind is still, the waves become calm, and we see the sun breaking through the clouds. Then we can breathe in the air that is crisp and clean with the fragrance that comes after the rain, and bask in God's faithfulness. Daily, if we let Him, the Holy Spirit will draw us to the Word, and remind us that God is faithful and will never forget us.

There will be an answer to our fervent prayers. There will be a time of hope and restoration. It is a matter of fact! What a wonderful promise! May we be restored with new encouragement today.

"We must meet the uncertainties of this world with the certainty of the world to come."

A.W. Tozer

# WEEK TWENTY-FIVE
## Keeping a Promise to a Friend

### *Perseverance*

*Now Mephibosheth the son of Saul came down to meet the king. And he had not cared for his feet, nor trimmed his mustache, nor washed his clothes, from the day the king departed until the day he returned in peace.*

*So it was, when he had come to Jerusalem to meet the king, that the king said to him, "Why did you not go with me, Mephibosheth?" And he answered, "My lord, O king, my servant deceived me. For your servant said, 'I will saddle a donkey for myself, that I may ride on it and go to the king,' because your servant is lame. And he has slandered your servant to my lord the king, but my lord the king is like the angel of God. Therefore do what is good in your eyes. For all my father's house were but dead men before my lord the king. Yet you set your servant among those who eat at your own table. Therefore what right have I still to cry out anymore to the king?"*

*So the king said to him, "Why do you speak anymore of your matters? I have said, 'You and Ziba divide the land.' " Then Mephibosheth said to the king, "Rather, let him take it all, inasmuch as my lord the king has come back in peace to his own house."*
**— 2 Samuel 19:24-30**

The story of Mephibosheth, son of Jonathan, grandson of King Saul, is a beautiful account of friendship and loyalty, and one of my favorites.

Saul's son, Jonathan, and David experienced a rare friendship, one that was loyal, committed, and carried them through some very hard times. David had promised Jonathan that no matter what happened, he would always look out for Jonathan's household.

When the tragic news of the deaths of Jonathan and Saul arrived, the community panicked. As they fled, Mephibosheth's nurse dropped him; his injuries left him lame in both feet. His life took a terrible turn and he was sent away to be raised in

*Keeping a Promise to a Friend* 75

exile. His name, which at birth meant *"he who strives for the Lord"* took on a new meaning; it has since been translated into various versions of *"he who spreads shame."*

When David finally secured his reign over Israel, he kept his promise to Jonathan by seeking out Mephibosheth, taking him into his home, and giving him a place at his table—a very significant act, implying that Mephibosheth was not just David's ward, but a member of his family. Politically, David had every right to destroy Mephibosheth. The young man was humbled by the king's generosity and couldn't believe that David would treat him like family. Mephibosheth loved David and was grateful for his mercy.

Later, David's son, Absolom, rebelled and caused David and the kingdom much grief. Abasalom led a military coup to take over kingdom, forcing David to leave Jerusalem. Who should meet David on the road, a little past the mountain, but Ziba, the servant of Mephibosheth. Leading two donkeys loaded with provisions, he cunningly offered them to David. When David asked the whereabouts of Mephibosheth, Ziba slandered his master and told David that Mephibosheth was staying behind in hopes of becoming king and restoring the family name, in David's absence. David believed the deception and hastily granted all of Mephibosheth's property to Ziba, which Ziba very "humbly" accepted. Such was the wickedness of Ziba that he took advantage of Mephibosheth's infirmity to steal his property.

This week's text takes place when King David returned to Jerusalem. Absalom was defeated and killed in battle. King David returned a victorious king, but a grieving father. When Mephibosheth came to meet the King, it was clear that he too was in some state of mourning. He had not washed his clothes or trimmed his beard or cared for himself at all since the king left Jerusalem.

Imagine David's pain. He was already weary from battle, grieving over the treachery and loss of his son, and now he sees Mephibosheth, who he had loved and treated like family. "Why did you not go with me, Mephiboshelth?" he asked. Mephibosheth explained Ziba's deception and how Ziba deliberately left without him, knowing that Mephibosheth was physically unable to make the journey alone. Mephibosheth's heart was broken to think he let David down, and he no longer felt worthy to be at the king's table.

David decided to restore Mephibosheth's possessions but

76    *Press On: 52 Reasons to Stay in the Race*

Mephibosheth's response is so remarkable that it touches my heart every time I read it: "Rather, let him [Ziba] take it all, inasmuch as my lord the king has come back in peace to his own house."

Mephibosheth's only concern was for the king. The king who had given him life, acceptance, respect, honor and love. This king who had run for his life for twenty years from Mephibosheth's own grandfather. This king who made good on a promise to his father, the father that Mephibosheth never really had a chance to know, for Jonathan was killed when Mephibosheth was only five years old. This king who was more of a father to him than his own flesh and blood.

In spite of the rumors and lies, the tragedy and heartache, Mephibosheth waited for his king to return, prepared to face anything. Because David had loved him so faithfully, Mephibosheth persevered in his love for David. He cast aside all care for himself, and was ready to sacrifice all his material possessions to find grace once again in the eyes of his king.

I pray that we too can persevere in the faith, so that return of the King of Kings is more important to us than our own physical comfort and occupies our thoughts day and night. We are going to be slandered, misunderstood, as well as ripped off in this life. That is a given. Mephibosheth was not preoccupied with bitterness, revenge or even self-pity. He only thought of the day when David would ride, victorious, back into Jerusalem, taking his rightful place upon the throne.

Isn't that how we should live and minister? Perseverance is lacking in the character of the twenty-first century saint, I fear. We need to learn to occupy until Jesus comes. Poor, lame Mephibosheth couldn't walk. But he was a very strong man. He was strong the way men need to be strong. He knew suffering, loss, and physical infirmity, but he was also a man of perseverance and a great encouragement to me. I pray that he is an encouragement to you as well.

*Keeping a Promise to a Friend*

"Faith, as Paul saw it, was a living, flaming thing leading to surrender and obedience to the commandments of Christ."

A.W. Tozer

# WEEK TWENTY-SIX
## *Seeing Jesus Through the Eyes of Paul*

---

### *Reality of God*

---

*For this reason I also suffer these things; nevertheless I am not ashamed, for I know whom I have believed and am persuaded that He is able to keep what I have committed to Him until that Day.* **—2 Timothy 1:12**

Don't you just love Paul the Apostle? I really wish I could have known this remarkable man in this life. His ability to communicate and his understanding of great spiritual principles are impressive. Though very well educated, he communicated effectively to the basic man on the street. He was zealous, but able to clearly and rationally share the Gospel. He was passionate about his faith, but still touched unbelievers without overwhelming them. He had access to heads of state and powerful leaders, but while in prison, he befriended Onesimus, the runaway slave, and led him to Christ.

Paul was never ashamed of the Gospel. He knew that God had ordained him to be a preacher, an apostle, and a teacher of the Gentiles. Because of this calling he suffered "these things," (imprisonment, persecution) but he never backed down or felt ashamed of this calling, because he knew the God in whom he believed, and he *knew* that God would guard and take care of all that Paul entrusted to Him until that Day.

This is living in the reality of God. Paul didn't say he knew *what* he believed, but rather *who*. He was secure in his personal revelation of the person of Jesus Christ. Not an historical Christ, or the doctrines of Christ. His confidence came from personally knowing God.

Paul never fell into the trap of the ministry becoming more important than the personal relationship. One of the great pitfalls of ministry is that we can become very familiar with what we believe, and begin to faithfully teach all the right doctrines and precepts, but we lose sight of the reality of the Person in whom we believe. How does it happen? How do we come to the place where our orthodoxy becomes more prominent than our personal relationship to Jesus? It happens very subtly, as programs replace inspiration, as corporation replaces devotion, as momentum replaces the Holy Spirit.

*Seeing Jesus Through the Eyes of Paul* 79

The people we lead must be fully persuaded that Christ is able to keep all they have committed to Him until that Day— the day they leave this earth or the day the Lord returns. They must know in *whom* they believe. If Jesus is real to us, He will be real to those we lead.

When you read the letters of Paul you cannot help but see Jesus through his eyes. Every time Paul wrote or spoke, he expressed the person of Christ. Paul's testimony and relationship with Jesus are recurring themes in the New Testament. Paul gave us his credentials, a snapshot of his life story, and his personal encounter with Jesus Christ on the road to Damascus. He described his personal revelation from Jesus Christ in the wilderness of Arabia for three years. He never lost sight of the *person* of Christ, whether he was preaching in prison, a crowd in the streets, or standing before a governor, a deputy, a king, or the emperor of Rome. A small group, or a huge crowd never altered his message. He simply shared about the One in whom he believed. The One who had set him free from orthodoxy and legalism. Jesus was very real to Paul and I believe He needs to be real to us.

I pray that no matter how long we are in the ministry, we would not fall away from the reality of God, and the reality of the person of Jesus Christ. And that we will always live in joyful gratitude for the day He set us free. I pray that we will experience the reality of the miraculous and the power of the Holy Spirit to lead us into new areas of ministry, and that we will know the joy of watching others come to faith and become excited about the Word of God. I pray that our ministries will be characterized by the centrality of Jesus Christ, meaningful worship, and plentiful opportunities to serve. This is something that we can all eagerly pursue, and in doing so, be confident that we will not lose the reality of God.

When we know God is real, even if He tarries another 50 years, we can press forward like our brother Paul.

# WEEK TWENTY-SEVEN
*Wide Awake and Free!*

## *Answers to Prayer*

*Peter was therefore kept in prison, but constant prayer was offered to God for him by the church. And when Herod was about to bring him out, that night Peter was sleeping, bound with two chains between two soldiers; and the guards before the door were keeping the prison.*

*Now behold, an angel of the Lord stood by him, and a light shone in the prison; and he struck Peter on the side and raised him up, saying, "Arise quickly!" And his chains fell off his hands. Then the angel said to him, "Gird yourself and tie on your sandals"; and so he did. And he said to him, "Put on your garment and follow me." So he went out and followed him, and did not know that what was done by the angel was real, but thought he was seeing a vision.*

*When they were past the first and the second guard posts, they came to the iron gate that leads to the city, which opened to them of its own accord; and they went out and went down one street, and immediately the angel departed from him. And when Peter had come to himself, he said, "Now I know for certain that the Lord has sent His angel, and has delivered me from the hand of Herod and from all the expectation of the Jewish people."*

*So, when he had considered this, he came to the house of Mary, the mother of John whose surname was Mark, where many were gathered together praying. And as Peter knocked at the door of the gate, a girl named Rhoda came to answer. When she recognized Peter's voice, because of her gladness she did not open the gate, but ran in and announced that Peter stood before the gate. But they said to her, "You are beside yourself!" Yet she kept insisting that it was so. So they said, "It is his angel." Now Peter continued knocking; and when they opened the door and saw him, they were astonished. —**Acts 12:5-16**

*Wide Awake and Free!* 81

Peter slept with two guards chained to his body. More guards watched the door to the cell. Squads of soldiers were in charge of keeping Peter in prison. Meanwhile, church gathered in constant prayer to God on Peter's behalf. They knew that Herod planned on executing Peter by the sword, in same manner as he executed James, on Passover.

What a challenge to one's faith! It seemed impossible to hope that Peter could somehow be delivered—especially after the way James died. They were all together at John Mark's mother's house. Praying. Hoping. What happened next is radically supernatural.

Peter slept soundly —as if he hadn't a care in the world. If that had been me, I don't think I would be sleeping! Peter either underestimated the seriousness of the situation, or he was a man of huge faith. I believe that the answer is a little of both. Answers to prayer come as a result of God's sovereign action, not because of us. Neither the faith of the one being prayed for nor of the ones doing the praying determines the outcome.

Peter had *learned* enough faith to be at peace and know that God was in control. (Maybe he learned his lesson on the Sea of Galilee, when Jesus slept through the storm.) Even so, both he and the church were completely surprised by God's radical answer to their prayers.

An angel came to the prison, hit Peter on the side of the head to wake him, and Peter's chains fell away. The two soldiers to whom he was chained never moved. The angel told him to hurry up and get dressed and follow him. Peter thought he was dreaming! They walked past the first and the second guard posts. No one stirred. The iron door to the prison opened on its own accord, and before he knew it, Peter was standing out on the street—and the angel disappeared.

Peter is now wide awake and a free man! After shaking the sleepiness and shock out of his brain, he declared, "Now I know...that the Lord has delivered me..." He understood that a miraculous act of God saved his life and set him free.

Peter headed straight to the house where everyone was praying. He knocked on the door and Rhoda answered. She recognized his voice but was so excited that she ran to tell everyone, but forgot to open the door. No one believed her. I can see them all sitting there, PRAYING, and yet shaking their heads, saying to poor Rhoda, "You're crazy! It can't be Peter – he's in prison. Why do you think we're praying here? Maybe it's his angel."

Peter kept on knocking until someone else opened the door and saw him. They were astonished, buzzing with shock! Peter had to shush them to share the story of how the Lord delivered him from prison.

Has this ever happened to you? You have been praying for something—something so impossible, that it is hard for you to believe God can answer it. Then God answers your prayer but you don't perceive it right away. I've done that. Incredibly, sometimes the answer has to keep knocking on my door for a while before I grasp the fact that God has answered prayers!

Pastor Don McClure said at the 2003 Calvary Chapel Pastor's conference[9], "Sometimes it takes all the faith we have to just believe in the promise." Like when God promised Israel, "For I will pour water on him who is thirsty, and floods on the dry ground; I will pour My Spirit on your descendants, and My blessing on your offspring..." (Isaiah 44:3). How many years do we labor and strive and pray and not see how God has answered that prayer for Israel and for all of us many times over?

I am so thankful that answers to prayer rely upon God alone. I know God wants us to believe in faith when we pray. He wants us to know that He is a rewarder of those who diligently seek Him, and it blesses Him to hear our petitions and intercessions. But I can't always muster up a huge faith, and it's encouraging to realize that I am not going to hinder God because of my limited ability to understand or believe.

Maybe your situation seems so impossible that it defies your imagination to think that God could possibly answer your prayer. But fortunately it does not matter how much faith you have, because, as Charles Spurgeon put it, "our faith is not in faith, but in the God upon whom our faith relies."[10] God answers prayer, in His own time and His own way. We simply hang onto whatever faith we have and trust Him with the outcome. The prayers of the church for Peter were answered, and once everyone recovered from the astonishment and shock, they all rejoiced, giving the Lord the glory.

May you receive the answer to your prayer today.

*Wide Awake and Free!*

"There are three indispensable requirements for a missionary:
    1. Patience
    2. Patience
    3. Patience."

*Hudson Taylor*

# WEEK TWENTY-EIGHT
## Leadership in Action

### Finishing Well

*Thus I cleansed them of everything pagan. I also assigned duties to the priests and the Levites, each to his service, and to bringing the wood offering and the firstfruits at appointed times. Remember me, O my God, for good!* **—Nehemiah 13:30-31**

Nehemiah is a great example of leadership in action. He is a role model for planning, prayer, delegation, faithfulness, integrity, and courage. Under his leadership, the rebuilding of the wall of Jerusalem was completed in fifty-two days, with gates hung, and gatekeepers, singers, and Levites appointed. When it was time for Nehemiah to return to his job as cupbearer to King Artaxerxes, he needed to delegate the responsibility of Jerusalem to sound leadership.

Nehemiah chose two men, his brother Hanani, and Hananiah, the leader of the citadel. Why did Nehemiah choose Hananiah? Not because he was already a leader or politically powerful, but because "...he was a faithful man and feared God more than many" (Nehemiah 7:1-2). What a wonderful reputation! I would like to have this written on my gravestone, because it would mean that I had finished my life well.

In our ministry, we can get so caught up in the work at hand that we lose sight of what is ultimately important to the Lord. Faithfulness, and a healthy respect and fear for God are two of the most important attributes needed to finish the job and finish well. Nehemiah recognized both traits in these men.

Faithfulness cannot be taught. It is a characteristic imparted by God to a yielded heart. Faithfulness is what marks the leader for great things and identifies a leader being developed by God. You can teach a leader to do the work of the ministry. You can teach the details of building, planning, and the principles of teaching, but you cannot make someone's heart faithful. God does that. Paul acknowledged that it was Jesus Christ who enabled him, counted him faithful, and put him into the ministry (1 Timothy 1:12). Timothy,

Tychicus, and Onesimus, are all described as being faithful. God sets an example for us throughout the Bible by demonstrating that He is faithful.

Hananiah was faithful, and he loved God. The Scriptures say his "fear of God" exceeded that of his peers, which I believe, in context, translates into love. How does one measure someone's love for God? How did Nehemiah identify this characteristic in Hananiah?

When people are serving the Lord, the attitudes of their hearts become visible. When you are around a person with a deep, abiding love for God, you can detect a tangible difference in that person. People like that are servants, and their love for the Lord is what motivates and constrains them. I have a friend who signs all of his correspondence with, "In His Grip." I like that word picture of a person who loves God, respects Him, and wants to live in Him. When this relationship with God is a practical reality in your life, it becomes a visible characteristic that affects everything about you.

Hananiah was the kind of leader that Nehemiah sought, to whom he could entrust the work of the ministry. It is my prayer that I will be found faithful in what the Lord has asked me to do. It is my prayer that my entire being will be gripped by God and my love for Him can manifest itself in serving others. It is my prayer that you will be encouraged today to finish well, to press forward, and to ask God to enable you to be faithful. I pray that you will allow Him to hold you in His grip.

# WEEK TWENTY-NINE
## Fisherman to Fisher of Men

---

### Call of God, Peter

*So when they had eaten breakfast, Jesus said to Simon Peter, "Simon, son of Jonah, do you love Me more than these?" He said to Him, "Yes, Lord; You know that I love You." He said to him, "Feed My lambs."*

*He said to again a second time, "Simon, son of Jonah, do you love Me?" He said to Him, "Yes, Lord; You know that I love You." He said to him, "Tend My sheep."*

*He said to him the third time, "Simon, son of Jonah, do you love Me?" Peter was grieved because He said to him the third time, "Do you love Me?" And he said to Him, "Lord, You know all things; You know that I love You." Jesus said to him, "Feed My sheep. Most assuredly, I say to you, when you were younger, you girded yourself and walked where you wished; but when you are old, you will stretch out your hands, and another will gird you and carry you where you do not wish."*

*This He spoke, signifying by what death he would glorify God. And when He had spoken this, He said to him, "Follow Me." Then Peter, turning around, saw the disciple whom Jesus loved following, who also had leaned on His breast at the supper, and said, "Lord, who is the one who betrays You?" Peter, seeing him, said to Jesus, "But Lord, what about this man?"*

*Jesus said to him, "If I will that he remain till I come, what is that to you? You follow Me."*

*Then this saying went out among the brethren that this disciple would not die. Yet Jesus did not say to him that he would not die, but, "If I will that he remain till I come, what is that to you?"* —**John 21: 15-23**

Peter figured he had pretty much failed as a disciple. Falling asleep in the Garden of Gethsemane, denying Jesus on the hardest day of His life, then watching his Lord die on the cross, helpless to stop it. It was a dark time for Peter.

He was happy and relieved to see Jesus risen from the dead when He appeared to the disciples in the upper room, and later by the sea shore. But for Peter, knowing he wasn't a very good disciple, decided to go back to what he knew so well and was always successful in doing. He turned away and simply said, "I am going fishing." Peter had finally come to the end of himself.

His friends went with him, but even after fishing all night, they caught nothing. It's really frustrating to fish and catch nothing, especially if fishing's your livelihood; if you know nothing else, you know how to catch fish! Peter must have been about as frustrated as can be at this point.

Then they saw someone standing on the shore, calling to them. *Children, have you caught any fish?* They didn't recognize the stranger who addressed these burly fishermen as "children," a term of endearment one would use for young children or dear friends.

"No," they answered, so Jesus told them to throw the net on the right side of the boat and then they'd catch some. They did it— and couldn't even pull in the nets, they were so full! One hundred-fifty-three large fish! Soon they all knew who the stranger on the shore was, as they recognized Jesus and prepared to have breakfast on the beach with Him.

After eating, Jesus and Peter entered into a dialogue concerning their relationship. "Do you love me more than these?" Jesus asked Peter. "These" represented something important to Peter —something he had to reconcile with his love for the Lord. Could the Lord have been talking about the fish, and being a fisherman? Or the others who followed Peter's lead and went fishing with him?

The terminology Jesus used asked Peter if he loved Jesus with *agape* love, the divine, sacrificial love that is the highest form of love. Peter responded that he loved Jesus with a *phileo* love, meaning brotherly affection. It was the best Peter could do at the time, the highest form of love he had to give. Peter was honest in his answer to the Lord, revealing himself to be an empty vessel, ready to be used by God.

Jesus used this conversation to call Peter to the ministry. He was asking Peter if he was ready to leave his nets and become a fisher of men. Jesus told Peter to "Feed my lambs," then asked Peter again, "Peter do you love (*agape*) me?"

Peter responded again, "Yes, Lord; You know that I love (*phileo*) you." Jesus said to him, "Tend my sheep." This is a term that could be translated "pastor" my sheep. Feed them, care for them, nurture them, pastor them. If you love Me more than anything or anyone else in your life, then be a shepherd to My flock.

The third time Jesus asked Peter "Do you love Me?" Jesus uses the Greek word *phileo* for love. Peter was grieved that the Lord would ask him for the third time, and responded, "Lord, You know all things; You know that I love you. "

Jesus answered him again, "Feed My sheep."

I believe Peter was grieved with this third question because he felt so unworthy, so inadequate, and that his love for Jesus was insufficient. But Peter didn't try to be phony, or more spiritual than he was. He was honest, responding with all that he had, as the Lord continued to reaffirm the call upon his life. Jesus was saying to Peter, "Your love for me is sufficient, but I am going to fill you with My love as you feed My lambs, tend My sheep, and feed My sheep." Then Jesus summed it all up in verse 19 when He simply said, "Follow Me." Peter was done operating in the flesh.

This is the key to ministry. My love for Him is natural, human love. The best I can do. His love for me is supernatural, and will give me the heart for ministry that no man can teach or make happen on his own.

Jesus will ask us all these questions and cause us to look within and be honest with Him. We say, "I love You with all that I am able, Lord." He affirms the call to feed and tend His sheep, then firmly says, "Follow Me."

That's when I can let go and truly let God fill me and use me for His glory. The people to whom I minister are not my lambs, or my sheep, but His. Sometimes we forget this and start creating programs and work that are beyond the call of Jesus.

I pray that we too will stop operating in the flesh, and allow Him to fill us with His love and empower us to carry out His command, "Feed My lambs. Tend My sheep. Feed My sheep."

*Fisherman to Fisher of Men*

"As soon as a man has found Christ, he begins to find others."

Charles Spurgeon

# WEEK THIRTY
## Blessed Are the Eyes That See the Things You See

---

### *Vision*

---

*Then He turned to His disciples and said privately, "Blessed are the eyes which see the things you see; for I tell you that many prophets and kings have desired to see what you see, and have not seen it, and to hear what you hear, and have not heard it."*
**—Luke 10:23-24**

The Bible tells us that believing is seeing.

Jesus sent seventy disciples out into the world to minister, in the power of the Holy Spirit and with the authority and power of the name of Jesus Christ. They returned rejoicing that the demons were subject to His name. They were thrilled by the experience of the power God manifested through them. "Lord, even the demons are subject to us in Your name," they said (Luke 10:17).

They were like any of us would be—excited to see so many miracles and mighty supernatural things happen—through them! Jesus shared in their joy, telling them, "I saw Satan fall like lightening..." But He also gently rebuked them. "Do not...rejoice that the spirits are subject to you, but rather rejoice because your names are written in heaven." It is not the power but the *source* of power that is significant.

He needed to remind the disciples of their priorities, but how delighted He was to see these spiritual babes, this band of new believers, blessed with such manifestations of the Spirit! "I thank You, Father, Lord of heaven and earth," He prayed, "that You have hidden these things from the wise and prudent and revealed them to babes."

Then when they were alone, He turned to His disciples and said, "Blessed are the eyes which see the things you see; for I tell you that many prophets and kings have desired to see what you see, and have not seen it and to hear what you hear, and have not heard it."

The disciples were experiencing and gaining spiritual knowledge beyond what many prophets and kings ever knew. Their belief in the person of Jesus and the power of His name gave them true spiritual vision. The prophets of old, Peter tells

*Blessed Are the Eyes That See the Things You See* 91

us later, prophesied the salvation and grace that would be poured out upon us, as well as the suffering of the Messiah and the glories that would follow. But they didn't really understand how, when, or even what would actually happen, in spite of their diligent studying (1 Peter 1:10-11). Now so much was being revealed to this band of spiritual novices, excited as children over what they were experiencing and learning!

Do you realize that we have the privilege to observe and participate in what others can only dream about? Christ is risen, the Holy Spirit is given, and we can go out in His name and His power because our names are written in heaven! Doesn't that make you rejoice like those early disciples who witnessed the power of God in action? The secret to vision is believing, and in believing you will see wondrous things.

I have always loved this passage of Scripture in Luke. Since the beginning of my conversion, I have seen miraculous healing, lives transformed, the demonic defeated, churches planted, and many more manifestations of the Holy Spirit. I can relate to the statement of Jesus to His disciples. I do believe that many have desired to see what I have seen, and to hear what I have heard. I am so blessed to have experienced the work of the ministry first hand.

Maybe you are reading this and saying that you haven't had this experience. That you are yearning to see and hear the things spoken about in the Scriptures. For years you have been studying and praying to see the power of God in action. Remember that the Lord has chosen to reveal these things to babes, not to "the wise and prudent." Be childlike in your faith, look into His wonderful face and say, *Lord I believe you are sending me in Your power and name.* Step out in believing faith and pray for the sick, teach the Word of God, go into the market place and find the lost. Then you will see and hear the things found in the Scriptures.

*Believing is seeing!* The concept of vision is multifaceted. One facet is to see the plan of action laid out in detail, the battle plan revealed step by step. Another type of vision is spiritual messages revealed through imagery. Another is simply the faculty of sight.

Vision requires two things to work: a vessel with the capacity to transfer images to the brain, and light. When Jesus healed the man blind from birth, He spat in the earth, rolled up the dirt and put it on the man's eye sockets. Then He told him to wash in the pool of Siloam. Jesus gave this man the instrument of physical sight; He made him a vessel capable of seeing. Jesus also said that He is the Light of the world (John 9:5). The instrument of sight, coupled with the Light, gave this man the capacity to see—and not just *physically* see, but to also see what only the Spirit can reveal.

The objective of Luke 10:23-24 is the capacity of sight, the ability, through believing faith, to see the kingdom of God advanced. To see the Lord of our salvation in a personal revelation, and to walk in His power.

May God grant you the ability to truly see.

"God's work done in God's way will never lack God's supplies."

Hudson Taylor

# WEEK THIRTY-ONE
## According to His Riches

### *Faithfulness of God*

*And my God shall supply all your need according to His riches in glory by Christ Jesus.*
**—Philippians 4:19**

Paul the apostle waited in a Roman prison for his final appeal, chained to two guards, down in a lower dungeon—and he was full of gratitude. He expressed his thankfulness in a letter to the church at Philippi for the aid they sent him in Thessalonica, and now in prison.

"I am full," he wrote to the Philippians, and you can hear the thankfulness in his words. He felt tremendously blessed and described their gifts as "a sweet-smelling aroma, an acceptable sacrifice, well pleasing to God." He rejoiced—not just for the gifts he received, but even more, he said, for the "fruit that abounds to your account." They were living and acting like real Christians, a great example of people in love with the Lord, and Paul knew they would be rewarded for their generosity.

Paul summed up his thank you letter to the Philippians with a statement of fact: **"And my God shall supply all your need according to His riches in glory by Christ Jesus."** He was confident and knew by personal experience the faithfulness of God.

Pastor Chuck Smith has often shared a personal story about this verse. Early in his ministry, Pastor Chuck worked for a grocery chain in the produce department. Money was tight and his union dues were due. He didn't have the money to pay the dues, and the union wouldn't let him work until they were paid. Of course he needed to work. He had bills to pay—including his union dues!

One night he couldn't sleep and so he got up and sat at his desk, going over his bills. They totaled $416.00—which he didn't have. He asked the Lord for wisdom on what to do. He had been offered a management position at the grocery chain, but that would mean quitting the ministry to work full time. He decided he had no choice but to call the grocery chain in the morning and accept the job.

The next morning the phone rang. Some friends of Pastor Chuck called to tell him that they felt impressed by the Lord to send him a check for his personal needs in the amount of $426.00. They wanted to tell him he could be looking for it in the mail. Pastor Chuck, elated and thrilled, danced around the kitchen with his wife, Kay, in celebration. This meant that he could pay all his bills and be debt free! What a wonderful thought.

Then, Chuck recalls, the Lord spoke to him in that still small voice, "Chuck, why are you so excited?"

Pastor Chuck responded, "Because my friend is sending the money to pay my bills."

"How do you know they are going to send that money?" the Lord responded.

"Surely he wouldn't call and tell me if he hadn't sent it," said Chuck, startled. "He is a man of his word!"

Then the Lord simply said, "Chuck, you had my Word last night and you weren't celebrating with Kay then. Isn't My Word more trustworthy than man's words?"

And Chuck remembered the words Paul wrote, the promise that God had spoken to his heart so many times before: ***"My God shall supply all your need according to His riches in glory by Christ Jesus."*** Pastor Chuck repented and asked God's forgiveness for trusting in a man's promise over and above God's promise. He never forgot this principle from God, and his ministry has always reflected this truth.[11]

God is faithful and true to His Word. He will provide for us. He will supply *all* of our need. I want to stress the word *all*. Not part of our need, not a great deal of our need, but <u>*all*</u> of our need. The text also says that He will supply all of our need *according* to His riches. "According" is a significant word. The Lord is not taking care of us "out of His riches" or "from His riches," but "*according*" to His riches. This means there is no end to His riches. They are infinite. You cannot deplete them. It's as if God gives us a blank check and we fill out the amount. No matter how many zeros you add, you will not deplete His account.

***"And my God will supply all of your needs according to His riches in glory by Christ Jesus."*** I don't think you can repeat those words too often. We need to memorize them, and burn the fact into our hearts and minds that the faithfulness of God is reliable and constant. He has given us His Word, the check is in the mail! We have reason to celebrate!

I pray that you will never doubt the faithfulness of God. Live and minister in the confidence that He will provide for your ministry and your personal needs. Whether it is just a few dollars or millions of dollars, the Lord is faithful to His Word.

*"And My God shall supply all of your need according to His riches in glory by Christ Jesus."*

"A state of mind that sees God in everything is evidence of growth in grace and a thankful heart."

*Charles Finney*

# WEEK THIRTY-TWO
## "What Have I Done to You?"

### Perseverance

*And it came to pass, when the Lord was about to take up Elijah into heaven by a whirlwind, that Elijah went with Elisha from Gilgal. Then Elijah said to Elisha, "Stay here, please, for the Lord has sent me on to Bethel." But Elisha said, "As the Lord lives, and as your soul lives, I will not leave you!"*

*So they went down to Bethel. Now the sons of the prophets who were at Bethel came out to Elisha, and said to him, "Do you know that the Lord will take away your master from over you today?" And he said, "Yes, I know; keep silent!" Then Elijah said to him, "Elisha, stay here, please, for the Lord has sent me on to Jericho." But he said, "As the Lord lives, and as your soul lives, I will not leave you!"*

*So they came to Jericho. Now the sons of the prophets who were at Jericho came to Elisha and said to him, "Do you know that the Lord will take away your master from over you today?" So he answered, "Yes, I know; keep silent!" Then Elijah said to him, "Stay here, please, for the Lord has sent me on to the Jordan." But he said, "As the Lord lives, and as your soul lives, I will not leave you!"*

*So the two of them went on. And fifty men of the sons of the prophets went and stood facing them at a distance, while the two of them stood by the Jordan. Now Elijah took his mantle, rolled it up, and struck the water; and it was divided this way and that, so that the two of them crossed over on dry ground. And so it was, when they had crossed over, that Elijah said to Elisha, "Ask! What may I do for you, before I am taken away from you?" Elisha said, "Please let a double portion of your spirit be upon me."* **—2 Kings 2:1-9**

Elisha was working hard in the field, with twelve yoke of oxen, when Elijah the Tishbite found him, took him by surprise, and changed his life forever.

Elisha and eleven other men were plowing a large field,

each with two oxen. Elisha plowed with the twelfth yoke. Most likely coming from an affluent family, Elisha carried many responsibilities, including the task of getting this field plowed. While in the midst of this back wrenching labor, Elijah walked up to him, threw his mantle (cloak) on him then walked away (1 Kings 19:19-21).

Elisha dropped his yoke, and ran after Elijah, calling, "Please let me kiss my father and my mother, and then I will follow you." He longed to answer the call the prophet had just placed upon him, but he felt the pressure of needing to take care of the physical and personal situations in his life first.

"Go back again, for what have I done to you?" Elijah responded. This was a call from God, not Elijah hiring Elisha, or asking him to come along. Elisha now answered to God, and needed to recognize that it was the Lord who was placing this mantle upon his shoulders.

Sometimes in ministry we can get confused concerning the call of God upon our lives. A person working in the ministry simply because it is a job is a hireling. Neither a Bible college degree nor an ordination certificate can make someone a minister. Only the divine call of God upon a man's life truly qualifies one for the ministry. Elijah's response to Elisha made it very clear that from that moment on, this was between Elisha and God. Elijah had obeyed what the Lord told him to do: "Elisha the son of Shaphat of Abel Meholah you shall anoint as prophet in your place" (1 Kings 19:16). As far as Elijah was concerned, his job was done.

Elisha understood. He went back (perhaps to say goodbye to his family), burned the yoke, slaughtered the oxen, boiled the meat, and gave it to the people to eat. "Then he arose and followed Elijah and served him," and never looked back. He set his heart upon this call, and began his role as a prophet by becoming a servant. I love it when I see people respond to the call of God. It's even more encouraging when they begin to develop a servant's heart. There are no shortcuts in ministry; the road is long and hard. The most vital lesson we can learn is that we cannot serve God if we don't have a servant's heart.

This brings us to this week's text. The time had come for the Lord to take Elijah from the earth, and for the prophecies to be fulfilled concerning this mighty prophet. Three times, Elijah gave Elisha the opportunity to stay behind, in Gilgal, Bethel, and Jericho. But Elisha was determined to be faithful to the call of God; he was determined to persevere in his service to Elijah and the Lord. Each time Elijah said, "Elisha, stay here, please..." Elisha adamantly refused, saying, "As the Lord lives and as your soul lives, I will not leave you!" This is a great example of perseverance because it is connected to the call of God upon a man's life, and how such a call requires a heart determined to be steadfast to the end.

As the two men crossed over the Jordan River, at the same point where the children of Israel had crossed over into the Promised Land from Mount Nebo, Elijah said to his young friend, "Ask! What may I do for you, before I am taken away from you?" Elisha's response is immediate and sincere. "Please let a double portion of your spirit be upon me."

"You have asked a hard thing," Elijah responded. "Nevertheless, if you see me when I am taken from you, it shall be so for you; but if not, it shall not be so."

They continued on their way, walking and talking together, when suddenly, in perhaps the most dramatic exit in history, Elijah is taken up in a chariot of fire with horses of fire, in a whirlwind. Wow!

Elisha, watching Elijah ascend, cried out, "My father, my father, the chariot of Israel and its horsemen!" as he tore his clothes into two pieces, a sign of mourning. Then he picked up the mantle that had fallen from Elijah, and returned to the bank of the Jordan. He struck the water with the cloak, and the water divided before him, so that he could cross over. The company of prophets from Jericho all recognized that the anointing of the spirit of Elijah was now upon Elisha.

The fruit of ministry will abound not to the talented, or the eloquent, or even the most intelligent, but to the one who perseveres in service.

"The Bible is either absolute, or it is obsolete."

Leonard Ravenhill

# WEEK THIRTY-THREE
## That Your Joy May Be Full

### *Reality of God*

*That which was from the beginning, which we have heard, which we have seen with our eyes, which we have looked upon, and our hands have handled, concerning the Word of life—the life was manifested, and we have seen, and bear witness, and declare to you that eternal life which was with the Father and was manifested to us—that which we have seen and heard we declare to you, that you also may have fellowship with us; and truly our fellowship is with the Father and with His Son Jesus Christ. And these things we write to you that your joy may be full. —1 John 1:1-4*

The longer I walk with the Lord, the more I discover that we can begin to lapse into a routine of service that dulls our sense of His reality. That's why I so appreciate John, the Beloved Disciple. He left us a great legacy of inspired Scripture that makes God real to me every time I read his writing. He gave us the Gospel of John, the Revelation of Jesus Christ, and three short letters, all demonstrating a powerful testimony of a man who knew and loved a very real God.

Chosen off the shores of the Sea of Galilee with his brother James, John became part of the inner circle of three disciples. During the Lord's three and a half years of public ministry, John had become perhaps His closest friend. He was not just a man following a spiritual leader, but had developed a personal, loving, and devoted relationship with Jesus. In fact, we see him reclining, leaning his head on Jesus like a close brother, during the last supper (John 13:23).

Everything changed the day Jesus was arrested, scourged, and crucified. John and Peter were there at the interrogation and mocking of Jesus. Then Peter became afraid and denied the Lord. Weeping bitterly, Peter ran off into the night. John was with Jesus to the end, the only one of the twelve present at the cross, wondering and grieving. Nothing would ever be the same.

The morning of the third day after Jesus' death, the women came to the disciples and reported that the stone had been moved from the tomb. Jesus' body was not there! Peter and John ran to the tomb, John arrived first, outrunning Peter. Peter immediately walked right into the tomb and saw (*thereo*, verse 6) the empty grave clothes. John followed Peter in, and Scripture says, "he saw (*eidon*) and believed" (John 20:8).

John came to believing faith at the vacant tomb when he saw the empty grave clothes. The Greek word *eidon*, used for the word "saw" in verse eight, means a complete understanding from what is perceived. This was where Jesus as God became real to John. This was the day John's personal relationship with Jesus was deepened by the revelation of the Resurrection, and John finally grasped the reality of God.

We, like John, can also have our own concept of who Jesus is, based on a tradition or family heritage. We can be raised in the church and have a sense of who God is, and we probably have some of it right. John knew Jesus for three and half years as a friend, a great teacher, and even as the Messiah. But not until the Resurrection, did he really possess a believing faith. Not until he saw (*eidon*) did he grasp the reality of having walked the earth with God incarnate!

This is why I believe he started out this letter (1 John) with the four verses above. This is the reason he wrote this letter at all. He wants others to come to a believing faith in the risen Christ, and not settle for what we think we understand. We must grab hold of the reality of God, the infallible reality that He is and is a rewarder of those who diligently seek Him.

The sect known as the Gnostics sought a deeper, hidden knowledge. Others were skeptical, acknowledging that He was a great teacher, or maybe even a prophet. But John said without reservation or hesitation, "Jesus is God."

"We were there, we touched Him, we ate with Him, we have seen Him live, we have seen Him die, and we have seen Him raised from the dead!" There was no doubt in John's mind or heart as he longed to share his story with others. ***And these things we write to you that your joy may be full.***

I have been in full time ministry now for almost 30 years. I know how easy it is to fall into the day-to-day routine of doing things our own way, because we forget the reality of God. Like the wicked servant who thought his Lord delayed his coming, so began to carouse and live for himself, there is a spiritual principle here that can affect the way we live. We must live in the reality of God's being and His imminent return, just as

104 *Press On: 52 Reasons to Stay in the Race*

John did. He wrote his Gospel and his letters, but he also wrote the Revelation of things to come.

Just as certainly as Jesus came the first time, He will come again as He promised. Living in the reality of His imminent return *will* affect our behavior. There are things we will not do, if we know the Father is at the door!

May we revisit the empty tomb from time to time to refresh our minds, "He is not here, He is risen!" May the reality of His imminent return spur us on to even more fruitful ministry.

"A Pharisee is hard on others and easy on himself, but a spiritual man is easy on others and hard on himself."

A.W. Tozer

# WEEK THIRTY-FOUR
## The Lord Always Listens

### *Answers to Prayer*

*And the Lord said, "Simon, Simon! Indeed, Satan has asked for you, that he may sift you as wheat. But I have prayed for you, that your faith should not fail; and when you have returned to Me, strengthen your brethren." —Luke 22:31-32*

If I had been sitting there in that small circle of friends surrounding Jesus, listening to Him talk about the kingdom to come, and someday sitting on thrones and judging the twelve tribes of Israel—and He suddenly turned to me and said, "Richard, Richard, Satan has asked to sift you like wheat"—I'd be a little worried!

But then Jesus said the most reassuring thing of all: "But I have prayed for you, that your faith should not fail..." Oh, to know that Jesus is directly praying for me! Jesus was trying to get Simon Peter's attention. But Peter, always impetuous, didn't quite tune in. Peter acted surprised and declared that he was ready to go to prison, and even die for the Lord. But Jesus continued, in spite of Peter's emotional outburst, and told him exactly what would happen, that Peter would deny Him three times before the cock crows.

I bet later, after it all happened as Jesus predicted, Peter looked back and remembered how Jesus promised to pray for him, and even gave him instructions for the future: "when you have returned to Me..." —not *if* but *when*— "strengthen your brothers." In one short exchange, Jesus warned Peter, described his downfall, promised him prayer support, and gave him a ministry. Jesus knew His prayers would be answered and that Peter would get back on track.

In our context of prayer, our frame of reference is always our prayers to the Lord. I know most of us feel like we don't pray long enough, or loud enough, or use the right words. Our focus is usually on our petitions and needs. But here, in Peter's story, we learn that Jesus prays for us—every day! One of the most exciting discoveries I made as a young Christian was in John 17:20, where Jesus says, "I do not pray for these alone, but also for those who will believe in Me through their word..." Jesus prays for me personally! The thought of me went through His mind as He prayed in the Garden of Gethsemane. Romans 8:34 and Hebrew 7:25 confirm that Jesus is at the right hand of the Father, interceding for us. He lives to make intercession for us.

What comfort that brings to my heart, to know that my Lord is praying for me. My prayers to Him daily are received in a joyful dialogue, and are to Him like a sweet fragrance of incense and sacrifice.

We all get discouraged at times, and wonder if God is even listening to our prayers. If we slip and backslide a bit, then we might think that God would definitely not want to hear from us and certainly won't answer any of our prayers when we're in such a state! But that kind of thinking just shows how short sighted we are on the dynamics of prayer. Sin does separate and hinder our fellowship, but the Holy Spirit is there to draw us back to a right relationship. Jesus is interceding on our behalf, to remove the blindness from our eyes, praying that we will cry out in honest repentance, asking forgiveness for our sin. A father is always looking down the road for the return of the prodigal child. His ear is always listening for the voice of his son calling for his dad.

We are all believers in Jesus because of the prayers of friends and family. *We are an answer to prayer.* There were five men whose salvation George Mueller regularly prayed for during his life. Two men received the Lord in George's lifetime, and three after he was gone.

Prayer is a fascinating part of our relationship with God. We pray to Him, He prays for us. Answers to prayer are consistent but our understanding of them is not. In Peter's case, Jesus gave him some insight into what he would face when his faith was tried, even preparing him for outcome: "When you have returned to Me, strengthen your brethren." Jesus' prayer for Peter is answered in the big picture, even though Peter still had to go through a time of testing. Peter denied the Lord, warmed his hands at the enemies' fire, and fell away for a time. But his faith did not fail in the end. His letters tell us of a love and faith that was steadfast and strong. And he was true to his word. He did ultimately die for the Lord.

We can be encouraged, knowing that our prayers and

petitions will be answered, because God answers prayer. And, in realizing that Jesus prays for us constantly! May we focus on the broader, supernatural aspects of prayer and look for answers to our prayers in the larger arena of life.

*When the time comes for you to die, you need not be afraid, because death cannot separate you from God's love."*

*Charles Spurgeon*

# WEEK THIRTY-FIVE
## Grow in Grace and Knowledge

### *Finishing Well*

*You therefore, beloved, since you know this before-hand, beware lest you also fall from your own steadfastness, being led away with the error of the wicked; but grow in the grace and knowledge of our Lord and Savior Jesus Christ. To Him be the glory both now and forever. Amen.* **— 2 Peter 3:17-18**

I believe Peter knew that this would be his last letter to the suffering church before he died a martyr's death. His words carry an urgency, much like Paul's last letter to Timothy. He urged the believers to be found by the Lord, when He returns for His church, "in peace, without spot, and blameless" (2 Peter 3:14). Peter also wanted to support what Paul wrote, as he too encouraged the church to stay strong and steadfast. Both apostles had to contend with untaught, unstable false prophets and deceptive teachers who twisted the Scriptures, destroying themselves, and leading others to destruction with them.

The verses above summarize this last message from Peter in a strong two-part exhortation. First, he lovingly exhorts his readers. He acknowledges their steadfastness, but reminds them that they too can fall, if they are deceived by the false teaching of wicked people. Resist the enemy, he urged. Don't fall from your steady walk with God. Then he continues in verse 18 with the positive exhortation to "grow in the grace and knowledge of our Lord and Savior Jesus Christ."

James imparted a similar message in James 4:7-8: "Resist the devil...draw near to God." It isn't the persecution of the church that causes people to fall away; it is the error of the wicked! The enticements of the world, the pleasures of sin for a season, the eroding of our faith, are what cause us to lose our footing.

Peter and Paul both finished well. They were both used mightily by God and reached thousands of people who were brought into the kingdom through their teaching and preaching of the Gospel. Literally hundreds of thousands have come to Christ through their writings! Which is even more amazing

*Grow in Grace and Knowledge*    111

and encouraging when you stop to think about who they were before they met Jesus. Both of them had very sketchy pasts.

Peter was a fisherman prone to impulsive acts and doing the wrong thing. More than once he had to be admonished. When the going got tough, he fell from his steadfastness, gave in to fear, and denied the Lord. Paul, formerly Saul of Tarsus, was a violently arrogant man, by his own admission (1 Timothy 1:13). As Saul, he persecuted the church ruthlessly, putting Christians in prison and even to death. He witnessed the stoning of Stephen, the first martyr for Christ. He was full of zeal but blind to the grace and the knowledge of Jesus Christ, until he encountered the Lord on the road to Damascus.

Both of these men were touched by the power of the Holy Spirit and transformed. They became strong, godly men, full of the love of God. Both of these men, although they had imperfect beginnings, finished well.

The exhortation to finish well, then, is connected to three things: *(1) resist the devil and the error of the wicked, (2) grow in the grace of Jesus Christ,* and *(3) grow in knowledge of Jesus Christ.*

Resisting evil is the application of obedience to what we know is right. Growing in grace is the Word of God dwelling in us (Colossians 3:16), teaching us (Titus 2:11-15), causing us to grow, and giving us strength to press on, knowing that God has forgiven us and will use us in spite of our failings. Growing in our knowledge of Jesus Christ happens through a personal relationship, developed by the Word, fellowship, and prayer.

Knowing the Lord is the key to fulfilling the first two conditions. I don't believe we can resist evil and understand grace without a deep knowledge of the Lord. There is a huge difference between knowing the President of the United States, knowing my pastor, and knowing my wife. We can know God in an intimate relationship that is closer than a brother, as close as a wife or husband. It is the most wonderful characteristic of the Holy Spirit's ministry to the believer. It is not a knowledge based on information about the person, but information *from* the person.

I love the old hymn, *In the Garden,* a portion of which says, "And He walks with me, and He talks with me, and He tells me I am His own. And the joy we share as we tarry there, none other has ever known."[12] The hymn depicts a personal walk in the garden with the Son of God, who speaks in precious terms of endearment. This is how we grow in the grace and the knowledge of the Lord Jesus Christ. We walk together, we talk together, through the course of the day. His Word is my lamp, and my anchor, and my rudder. Isn't it amazing how the Word of God can be all these things to me?

Finally my brethren, be strong, be faithful, and finish well.

"What good are Greek, commentaries,
insight, gift, and all the rest,
if there is no heart for Christ?"

*Jim Elliot*

# WEEK THIRTY-SIX

## *"Who Are You, Lord?"*

---

### *Call of God, Paul*

---

*And when we all had fallen to the ground, I heard a voice speaking to me and saying in the Hebrew language, "Saul, Saul, why are you persecuting Me? It is hard for you to kick against the goads."*

*So I said, "Who are You, Lord?"*

*And He said, "I am Jesus, whom you are persecuting. But rise and stand on your feet; for I have appeared to you for this purpose, to make you a minister and a witness both of the things which you have seen and of the things which I will yet reveal to you. I will deliver you from the Jewish people, as well as from the Gentiles, to whom I now send you, to open their eyes, in order to turn them from darkness to light, and from the power of Satan to God, that they may receive forgiveness of sins and an inheritance among those who are sanctified by faith in Me." —* **Acts 26:14-18**

Imprisoned for sedition in Caesarea on trumped up charges by angry Jewish leaders, the apostle Paul had appealed his case to Rome, taking advantage of his status as a Roman citizen. King Agrippa, the puppet Jewish king under the Romans, and his wife Bernice (who was also his sister) had just arrived in Caesarea to greet the new Roman governor of Judea, Festus.

Festus wasn't given any specific charges against this interesting prisoner he inherited from the previous governor, so discussed the case with Agrippa, who finally said, "I would like to hear the man myself."

So Paul found himself in just the kind of situation he loved best. Standing before people who *ask* him to speak, giving him the opportunity to share the Gospel and his testimony of Jesus Christ.

Paul opened with an eloquent greeting to King Agrippa, then began to tell of his life as a Pharisee and a persecutor of those who followed Jesus of Nazareth. He had done just what the Pharisees were doing to him, and worse. He described his rage, his desire to hurt, imprison, and even put to death these

*"Who Are You, Lord?"* 115

new believers. He forced them to blaspheme, scoured the synagogues looking for people to punish. He was so obsessed that he pursued and persecuted them even in foreign cities.

In the midst of his zealous frenzy, while journeying to Damascus, everything changed, he told the court. "O king, along the road I saw a light from heaven, brighter than the sun." He and his companions fell to the ground, he said, when he heard a voice speaking to him in the Hebrew language, "Saul, Saul, why are you persecuting Me? It is hard to kick against the goads."

"Who are you, Lord?" Paul responded.

"I am Jesus, whom you are persecuting. But rise and stand on your feet; for I have appeared to you for this purpose, to make you a minister and a witness both of the things which you have seen and of the things which I shall yet reveal to you. I will deliver you from the Jewish people, as well as from the Gentiles, to whom I now send you. To open blind eyes, in order to turn them from darkness to light, and from the power of Satan to God, that they may receive forgiveness of sins and an inheritance among those who are sanctified by faith in Me."

What an amazing call of God! The whole encounter left Paul blind for three days, until a disciple in Damascus named Ananias prayed for him, and Paul not only received his sight, but was also baptized and filled with the Spirit. Paul had been called by God into the ministry in one of the most dramatic encounters ever recorded, and he responded by immediately going out and preaching Jesus, the Son of God.

"Therefore, King Agrippa," he said, summing up his testimony, "I was not disobedient to the heavenly vision..."

The call of God upon a person's life is very specific—and is meant to cost you everything! In examining the call of God upon your life, can you look back and identify when it took place? Can you recall what the Lord said to you when He invited you to be His servant? I believe in most cases, you can mark that day. The call of God can take place in the shower, on the job site, or in the church sanctuary. It is manifested in the voice of God impressing upon you what He wants you to do with your life. It can be quiet and subtle, it can be dramatic and obvious. But it will be specific and clear.

When the Lord called me, it was during a Sunday evening service of Calvary Chapel of San Diego, in the North Park Theater, as I recounted in Week Eight. Pastor Mike MacIntosh was leading the Bible study when the Lord spoke to my heart, saying, "Richard, I want you to feed my sheep." Everything from that day forward was in preparation for the day the Lord would call me into full time ministry.

Young Samuel responded to the Lord's call to become a prophet with a quick, "Speak, for your servant hears!" (1 Samuel 3:10). We too, eager and excited, often respond with limited understanding, as we are just beginning to recognize His voice. Some receive a verse of scripture that jumps off the page and into their hearts. For me, it was Jeremiah 3:15, which God gave me early in 1977: *"And I will give you shepherds according to My heart, who will feed you with knowledge and understanding."* My friend Walter Thompson and I were serving as ushers at Calvary Chapel San Diego (later to become Horizon Christian Fellowship), in the North Park theater. We were each teaching a home group in the Mira Mesa area when the Lord spoke to me through this verse one night. It confirmed that He had put a call upon my life, and I determined that every decision I made from that day forward would be in line with this call. Like Paul, I was not disobedient to the heavenly vision. Four years later in June of 1981 I was ordained as a minister of the Gospel at Calvary Chapel Poway, California. Oswald Chambers says the call of God is universal, but only those that are called hear it.[13]

May we all hear the call upon our lives and remain obedient to the heavenly vision.

"Faith never knows where it is being led,
but it loves and knows the One who is leading."

Oswald Chambers

# WEEK THIRTY-SEVEN
## *Four Young Men of Passion*

---
### *Vision*
---

*Then the secret was revealed to Daniel in a night vision. So Daniel blessed the God of heaven. Daniel answered and said: "Blessed be the name of God forever and ever, for wisdom and might are His. And He changes the times and the seasons; He removes kings and raises up kings; He gives wisdom to the wise And knowledge to those who have understanding.*

*He reveals deep and secret things; He knows what is in the darkness, and light dwells with Him. "I thank You and praise You, O God of my fathers; You have given me wisdom and might, and have now made known to me what we asked of You, for You have made known to us the king's demand."*
**—Daniel 2:19-23**

Daniel and his companions were young men when the Babylonians took them into captivity—not more than boys, really. The Chaldeans were specifically looking for young, noble men with potential to learn. Daniel and his friends fit the description, for God had blessed them with wisdom, knowledge, and skill in literature—perfect candidates to serve as wise men in the court of the king. They were given new names, and taught the language and literature of the Chaldeans. Their stature grew as the king discovered that they were more gifted than all the astrologers and magicians in his kingdom. He would soon learn that Daniel also had the gift for understanding visions and dreams.

A deeply disturbing dream troubled King Nebuchadnezzar. He couldn't sleep and his anxiety grew as he struggled to understand the dream's meaning. He called upon his magicians, astrologers, sorcerers, and the Chaldean people to help him. But he was so superstitious that, rather than tell them the dream and ask for interpretation, he demanded that they tell him the dream and the meaning—or be killed. His counselors protested saying, "There is not a man on earth who can tell the king's matter...It is a difficult thing that the king requests, and there is no other who can tell it to the king except the gods...."

In his rage, the king issued a decree for all wise men to be put to death—including Daniel and his companions. "Why is this decree so urgent?" Daniel asked the captain of the king's guard. When he learned the seriousness of the situation, Daniel went to the king and asked for time to interpret the king's dream.

Daniel, Hananiah (Shadrach), Mishael (Meshach), and Azariah (Abed-Nego) came together and sought the mercies of the God of heaven—their lives depended on being able to solve this mystery. During the night, the secret was revealed in detail to Daniel in a vision. Daniel immediately praised God, and the verses above are his prayer of thanksgiving.

Daniel's was a classic vision. A vision from God especially involves three supernatural gifts of the Holy Spirit working in concert: the Word of knowledge, the Word of wisdom, and prophecy. God is omniscient. He knows all. He is the source of all knowledge. A fragment of His knowledge is revealed in a vision; wisdom gives insight as to how that knowledge is applicable, how it affects persons, places, or events. The interpretation of this knowledge and wisdom is proclaimed through the spoken word of prophecy. That is exactly what Daniel experienced as he stood before King Nebuchadnezzar and declared, "There is a God in heaven who reveals secrets...." Then he proceeded to tell the king all that he needed to know.

The prophet Joel spoke about the last days, when young men will see visions, and old men will dream dreams. This is a miraculous demonstration of the power of the living God. This is something to desire in our spiritual lives!

We need vision in the sense of purpose and goals, but we also need to see visions. There is a distinction. One vision gives us a clear plan as the Lord reveals His heart for a country, or a city, or a particular work, and unveils a course of ministry. The other type of vision is what we see in the book of Daniel. A supernatural, visual revelation involving the three gifts of the Holy Spirit. Peter witnessed a dramatic vision on the rooftop of Simon the Tanner's house, of unclean animals being presented to him for food. God revealed to Peter through this vision a principle for reaching out to the Gentiles.

In our ministries we need to ask the Lord to give us that same wisdom, knowledge, and understanding of visions and dreams as he gave to Daniel and his companions. When that

120    *Press On: 52 Reasons to Stay in the Race*

happens, God is glorified and we are blessed to be used as a vessel for His glory.

I encourage you to ask the Lord for vision, and be open to what He reveals. It could be a new vision for ministry, or a dramatic answer to a perplexing question, or a much needed revelation of divine truth. Read the verses above again right now (Daniel 2:19-23), and meditate on them for a while. Remember. Daniel asked, and the Lord answered. *"You have given me wisdom and might, and have now made known to me what we asked of You,"* he said.

May the Lord encourage you in your walk today, and may God grant you vision for your life and ministry!

"The man, the whole man lies behind the sermon. Preaching is not the performance of an hour. It is the outflow of a life."

E.M. Bounds

# WEEK THIRTY-EIGHT
## Coming Back to Grace

### *Faithfulness of God*

*I thank my God always concerning you for the grace of God which was given to you by Christ Jesus, that you were enriched in everything by Him in all utterance and all knowledge, even as the testimony of Christ was confirmed in you, so that you come short in no gift, eagerly waiting for the revelation of our Lord Jesus Christ, who will also confirm you to the end, that you may be blameless in the day of our Lord Jesus Christ. God is faithful, by whom you were called into the fellowship of His Son, Jesus Christ our Lord.*
**—1 Corinthians 1:4-9**

In our Christian walk we can fall into two extreme positions. We can become legalistic, self-righteous, critical, and lacking in love or joy. Or, we go the other way and become carnal, spiritually lazy, disrespectful, self-seeking, and void of spiritual power. The enemy loves it when believers fall into these extremes, because they both lead to barrenness and unfruitfulness.

Paul faced a troubled church in the Corinthians. He need to guide them back to a solid "straight and narrow" walk with the Lord before they continued teetering off into the extremes. His greeting to the Corinthian believers in the first nine verses of 1 Corinthians is very encouraging, including his heartfelt prayer (verses 4-9), from which we can glean several characteristics of the Corinthian believers.

They were a people greatly enriched by the grace of God, which influenced the way they spoke, their grasp of knowledge—everything! The testimony of their faith in Christ was an observable part of their life.

We know that this letter was a strong exhortation from Pastor Paul. The Corinthians had issues. They were divided, abusing the gifts of the Holy Spirit, and becoming more and more carnal. But Paul was smart and sensitive in dealing with the church. He knew the importance of recognizing the good in a situation. In the past, the Corinthians had a reputation for being fornicators, idolaters, adulterers, thieves, drunkards,

*Coming Back to Grace* 123

extortioners ...and that's just a partial list (1 Corinthians 6:9-11)! The fact that they were now changed by Christ is something to acknowledge, which Paul does. The fact that no matter where we come from, or what we have done, we can be changed, enriched, and confirmed blameless in the day of our Lord Jesus Christ is cause for rejoicing! The conclusion of the matter is enthusiastically expressed by Paul at the end of his prayer: "God is faithful, by whom you were called into the fellowship of His Son, Jesus Christ our Lord."

We can always rely upon the faithfulness of God! The Corinthians had come from a very carnal and dark past, but they were changed and transformed by the grace of God. As they fell into various sins and mistakes, God was faithful in bringing this letter from Paul, to bring correction and restoration. Just as God is faithful to love us and call us into the fellowship of His Son, and He is also faithful to bring what ever is needed to keep us on the right path.

God loves His children, and because of His love for us, He disciplines us. When He sees us falling into those extremes of legalism and carnality, He is faithful to bring us from the letter of the law to grace. He is faithful to humble us and soften our self-righteous hearts. He is faithful to fill us with a joy unspeakable that the world cannot give. He is faithful to draw us into the pursuit of holiness that dissipates the carnality and fills us with spiritual power. This is the faithfulness of God that Paul experienced first hand.

Intimacy with God is a wonderful by-product of receiving His *agape* love. *Agape* love creates within us a desire to respond with love for God, love for the people around us, and gives us a longing for others to experience this love as well. Paul knew this love, and had such a burden for the believers he saw struggling or being lured into dangerous positions, that he was controlled, compelled, by the love of Christ to write, preach, exhort, pray, encourage, discipline—whatever was needed (2 Corinthians 5:14) to help these brothers and sisters avoid the pitfalls of carnality or legalism. Paul's passion to preach Christ consumed him; he wanted to know Christ and the fellowship of His suffering (Philippians 3:10). He wanted others to know the joy and the power of knowing Him. He wanted others to count on the faithfulness of God.

God always wants the best for you. Every action and consequence is for our benefit and growth. We don't always understand that when we are going through the refining process. But as Paul explained to Timothy, "If we are faithless, He remains faithful; He cannot deny Himself" (2 Timothy 2:13).

May we recognize and experience the faithfulness of God as He works in our lives to keep us close to Him.

"Few things are impossible to diligence and skill. Great works are performed, not by strength, but perseverance."

Samuel Johnson

# WEEK THIRTY-NINE
## Enjoying the Ride

### Perseverance

*Therefore, having been justified by faith, we have peace with God through our Lord Jesus Christ, through whom also we have access by faith into this grace in which we stand, and rejoice in hope of the glory of God. And not only that, but we also glory in tribulations, knowing that tribulation produces perseverance; and perseverance, character; and character, hope.*

*Now hope does not disappoint, because the love of God has been poured out in our hearts by the Holy Spirit who was given to us.* **—Romans 5:1-5**

Peace requires perseverance. But peace is also a gift from God, a fruit of His Spirit, and the apostle Paul diligently taught the early believers what it takes to experience peace with God and joy in the midst of tribulations. He emphasized the important principle that one cannot obtain the peace *of* God, without first entering by faith into peace *with* God.

His letter to the Romans carefully explains how a person, in becoming a Christian, obtains peace *with* God, and also has access to the peace *of* God. "Therefore having been justified by faith, we have peace with God through our Lord Jesus Christ," Paul wrote.    To be justified means to be declared righteous. When we place our faith in the One who died in our place, God declares us righteous.  Our sins are gone, the weight is gone, and we are no longer aliens from God, no longer enemies of God. We are at peace *with* God. Now, as His children, our lives will be radically altered by the peace *of* God. Paul gives us two examples in his letters to the Colossians and Philippians:

**"And let the peace of God rule in your hearts, to which also you were called in one body; and be thankful"** **(Colossians 3:15-16).**

**"Be anxious for nothing, but in everything by prayer and supplication, with thanksgiving, let your requests be made known to God; and the peace of God, which surpasses all understanding, will guard your hearts and minds through Christ Jesus"** **(Philippians 4:6-7).**

*Enjoying the Ride* 127

This peace rules in your heart when you are saved. This peace guards our hearts and minds against anxiety and fear, to a degree that is beyond human understanding. Through Jesus, we can take everything to God in prayer, cast our worries upon Him, and know peace.

Paul is preparing us here for what is to come. First he assures us that we are at peace with God—then he reminds us that as believers "... we glory in tribulations, knowing that tribulations produce perseverance (endurance), and perseverance, character and character, hope." You're at peace, but that doesn't mean things aren't going to be hard. It's hard for me to honestly say I glory in tribulation. But when I read these verses I am encouraged, because I understand that tribulation shapes my character and builds endurance.

Life gives us examples of these spiritual principles now and again. I have been riding a road bike now for a little over two years, with a group of five to six men from church, on Saturday mornings. When the weather permits, we sometimes ride two or three times a week. When I started, I could only ride a short distance. But each week, as I persevered, I grew a little stronger. Biking is not so much a sport of great physical strength, but rather of endurance and stamina. Just recently, I was able to ride forty-two miles on a three-hour ride—and I really got what Paul meant by glorying in tribulation! The ride was hard. I was extremely uncomfortable, tired, and thirsty. But then I would look around, view the beautiful countryside, and allow myself to enjoy ride. And when I made it, when I finished those forty-two miles, it was exciting and exhilarating!

This is what Paul had in mind when he said we can glory in our tribulations because we know that tribulations cause us to persevere, and perseverance builds our character, and gives us hope for the future. Perseverance leads to proven character. My riding group is working up to a longer ride next summer—seventy-five miles in a five-hour ride. I look forward to more character building.

I really like the way the Amplified Bible describes this process:

**"And endurance (fortitude) develops maturity of character (approved faith and tried integrity). And character [of this sort] produces [the habit of] joyful and confident hope of eternal salvation." (Romans 5:4 AMP).**

We can approach our relationship to God with joyful

abandon, because we can be at peace, and we know that the trials we endure will make us stronger. We have hope in something very real!

Hang in there and enjoy the ride!

"Beware in your prayers, above everything else, of limiting God, not only by unbelief, but by fancying that you know what He can do."

Andrew Murray

# WEEK FORTY
## *When I Put My Hands in His Wounds*

---
### *Reality of God*
---

*And after eight days His disciples were again inside,
and Thomas with them. Jesus came, the doors being
shut, and stood in the midst, and said, "Peace to you!"
Then He said to Thomas, "Reach your finger here, and
look at My hands; and reach your hand here, and put
it into My side. Do not be unbelieving, but believing."
And Thomas answered and said to Him, "My Lord and
my God!" Jesus said to him, "Thomas, because you
have seen Me, you have believed. Blessed are those
who have not seen and yet have believed."*
**— John 20: 26-29**

Thomas was a practical man who refused to believe something just to conform to the crowd. He was absent from the upper room when Jesus appeared the first time after the Resurrection. I wonder where Thomas was that evening? Why do you think Thomas would miss such an important gathering of the disciples? Pastor Matthew Henry speculates that he was ill, or still mulling over his sinful nature, or that his natural skepticism made him reluctant to go along with the disciples. Whatever the reason, he missed the Lord!

That is always the result of being out of fellowship. We miss what the Lord is doing as He ministers to the church. Jesus had appeared to His discouraged and fearful disciples, and "breathed on them and said, 'Receive the Holy Spirit'" (John 20:21). What a wonderful gathering! Thomas missed out on the moment Jesus commissioned and empowered His disciples.

Sometimes we can get so caught up in working for the ministry that we neglect to keep ourselves in fellowship, where we are hearing the Lord and being ministered to as well. I know Christian workers who are at church a lot, but rarely *in* church or Bible studies and prayer meetings. Sometimes we can hide out in our ministry positions and start feeling like church is a chore. Jon Courson nicely reminds us, "As Christians we don't *have* to go to church, we *get* to go to church."

The lyrics of a favorite worship song say it all:

*When I Put My Hands in His Wounds* 131

**"As we gather may your Spirit move among us, as we gather, may we glorify Your name,**

**Knowing well that as our hearts begin to worship, we'll be blessed because we came."[14]**

When the disciples tried to tell Thomas about the Lord's appearance, he looked at the other ten and declared, "Unless I see in His hands the print of the nails, and put my finger into the print of the nails, and put my hand into His side, I will not believe." Doubting Thomas (as he came to be known in church history) needed physical, tangible proof that Jesus had really risen from the dead.

Eight days later they gathered again; this time Thomas was present. Jesus again appeared in their midst with the greeting, "Peace to you!" Then He immediately turned His attention to Thomas telling him to "Reach your finger here. And look at My hands; and reach your hand here and put it in My side."

Jesus never condemned Thomas for his skepticism. He simply exhorted him to do what he needed to do to believe, encouraging Thomas, "Do not be unbelieving, but believing."

I appreciate this about God. We can be honest with Him, and ask the hard questions. We can investigate our faith without fear, because it will measure up. No matter how deep we probe, or how much we question, God will stand the test. Some Christians are intimidated by learned, so-called educated men who claim that Christians have a "blind" faith, and believe without evidence. That is absolutely not true. We have seen in the Scriptures where Jesus presented Himself alive after many infallible proofs (Act 1:3). We have looked at 1 John 1-4 where the apostle states, "that which we have seen and heard we declare to you," and 2 Peter 1:16, which declares, "We did not follow cunningly devised fables when we made known to you the power and coming of our Lord Jesus Christ, but were eyewitnesses of His majesty." Eyewitness accounts, plus historical and archeological proof abounds.

Thomas, face to face with the reality of Jesus and His Resurrection, cried out with heartfelt conviction, "My Lord and my God." Thomas demonstrated powerful, believing faith. We can follow his example by asking the Lord to reveal Himself to us in a way that we can understand. The Holy Spirit can bring the Scriptures to life and teach us to apply them in ways that will change us forever! And we never know how God will use what we learn.

132    *Press On: 52 Reasons to Stay in the Race*

Centuries later, Thomas' dramatic exclamation in verse 28 brought a Mr. Peter Barnes to faith in Christ.[15] Mr. Barnes had been a Jehovah's Witness for over 40 years, reaching the level of district supervisor in the organization. When questions about this Jesus began to cast doubt in his mind, he began to read the Bible instead of just the Jehovah's Witnesses publications. One day he discovered this verse and realized that Jesus did not correct Thomas in his declaration, "My Lord and my God." Jesus received Thomas' recognition of Him as God, and his worship. Just as Thomas came to a believing faith, so did Peter Barnes. He realized that he had been deceived for forty years as he placed his finger in the nail prints of Jesus' hands, and his hand into His side, and he was saved. He has had an amazing ministry of teaching and reaching other Jehovah's Witnesses ever since.

Jesus is real and I pray that you will come into the fellowship of the brethren today, and be refreshed by the reality of God. Maybe you have been discouraged and doubting the Lord. Today is the day to get back into fellowship, to touch Him, and allow Him to restore your faith.

*When I Put My Hands in His Wounds*  133

"The golden rule for understanding in spiritual matters is not intellect, but obedience."

Oswald Chambers

# WEEK FORTY-ONE
## Outnumbered and Outgunned

---
### *Answers to Prayer*
---

*Then David said to the Philistine, "You come to me with a sword, with a spear, and with a javelin. But I come to you in the name of the Lord of hosts, the God of the armies of Israel, whom you have defied. This day the Lord will deliver you into my hand, and I will strike you and take your head from you. And this day I will give the carcasses of the camp of the Philistines to the birds of the air and the wild beasts of the earth, that all the earth may know that there is a God in Israel. Then all this assembly shall know that the Lord does not save with sword and spear; for the battle is the Lord's, and He will give you into our hands."*
**—1 Samuel 17:45-47**

The battle of David and Goliath, certainly one of the most famous stories to influence our culture, is historically accepted by Christians, Jews, and Moslems alike, and has become the proverbial expression of any small force challenging a larger one. In business, when a small company faces off against a large corporation, the story of David and Goliath is evoked. Military battles, where an army is heavily outnumbered and outgunned by the enemy, are described in David and Goliath terms. The story of the young shepherd boy defying the giant Philistine has long inspired believers to attempt the impossible, and to put our faith and confidence in our God.

In the ancient days of battle, before weapons of warfare were invented which allowed man to destroy his enemy without actually having to see him, battles were fought hand to hand, resulting in massive bloodshed and the loss of thousands of lives. Armies often designated a champion, the fiercest fighter and the most skilled in the art of war, to fight for them. He was usually trained for battle from a very young age. The champion of one army would step out to face the champion from the other army, and the one who emerged victorious could declare victory for his entire army.

This is the scene in 1 Samuel 17. The Philistine army sent

*Outnumbered and Outgunned* 135

Goliath, a giant of a man who stood over nine feet tall, to challenge the Israelites. Trained to fight from a young age, his coat of mail body armor alone weighed 125 pounds. With a javelin on his back, a strong helmet on his head, he carried a spear with a 15-pound iron spearhead. His sword strapped to his side, he kept his hand free for action by having a man walking in front of him carrying his shield. Goliath from Gath was intimidating! He taunted, mocked, and challenged Israel for days to send a champion to fight him.

David, a small, young shepherd boy, had been assigned to bring dried grain and bread to his older brothers on the battlefield. David had been trained to only do one thing in his life and that was to take care of a flock of sheep. In his solitary life as a shepherd, David spent a lot of time contemplating, praying, worshiping, and growing close to the Lord. David probably spent more time with the Lord in his young life than Goliath spent learning to fight. David learned to be faithful, courageous, and to trust in the living God.

He was outraged to see this Philistine defy the armies of the living God, and he stepped up to the challenge. His brothers were angry and accused him of being prideful. Others doubted him; King Saul tried to talk him out of it. But David was determined, standing on his faith. "The Lord...will deliver me," he declared.

What an incredible sight it must have been to see this young boy, as he took off the armor Saul tried to give him, and stepped out with a sling and five stones to face a heavily armored giant!

There is no way in the physical universe that David could defeat this giant Philistine. Impossible! But that didn't deter him, as he answered Goliath's disdain: "You come to me with a sword, with a spear, and with a javelin, but I come to you in the name of the Lord of Hosts, the God of the armies of Israel, whom you have defied. This day the Lord will deliver you into my hand, and I will strike you and take your head from you. And this day I will give the carcasses of the camp of the Philistines to the birds of the air and the wild beasts of the earth, that the earth may know that there is a God in Israel."

David's final words to the Philistine, however, are the key to our devotion this week: ***"The Lord does not save with sword and spear; for the battle is the Lord's...."*** (verse 47). Please underline all three of these verses in your Bible, but double underline those words. This is our lesson for a lifetime.

136 *Press On: 52 Reasons to Stay in the Race*

We are going to face many Goliaths in our lifetime. Some will be in the work place, some will be in our families. And I can promise you, there will be Goliaths in the ministry. The world can come against us with all the armor of Goliath and seem so huge and intimidating that the odds appear insurmountable. But this is the exact scenario that glorifies the Lord. He does not save with sword or spear. The battle is the Lord's and He will deliver victory into our hands.

The years David spent worshiping the Lord prepared him for this battle, and the battles that followed throughout the rest of his life. The lessons David learned tending sheep made him a valiant warrior and man of faith. Pastor and Bible teacher David Gusik said at a Pastor's conference, in January of 2003, "God receives greater glory when man is involved with the battle and victory."[16]

At first that statement doesn't make sense to some people. But his point was, that when we try, through our own logic, skill, and cunning to win a battle, and we fail, then God steps in and does the impossible. God could have easily zapped Goliath and gotten rid of him, but God receives greater glory when men are involved and face an impossible situation. There are things we simply cannot do on our own, no matter how armed or prepared we might be. There will be moments in each of our lives when we are compelled to face a Goliath, and in so doing, risk everything and abandon ourselves completely to the God who answers prayer.

Let us pray today and watch the Lord fight our battles!

"To teach in order to lead others to faith is the task of every preacher and of each believer."

Thomas Aquinas

# WEEK FORTY-TWO
## When the Lord Rejoices

### *Finishing Well*

*"I have no greater joy than to hear that my children walk in truth."—3 John 1:4*

I love this verse. These words of John, "I have no greater joy..." speak to me as a pastor. There is a wonderful joy that fills my heart when I hear that the people I minister to are doing well in the Lord, and walking in the truth. John communicates much of this same joy in his letters to the church.

The Book of 3 John is a very short but powerful letter, one of three written about the same time (late 90s AD) by John, the beloved disciple. Each letter emphasizes a particular point. The first letter exhorts us to have fellowship with God, the second letter strongly urges the believer to avoid false teachers, and the third letter encourages believers to band together in fellowship to help one another "walk in truth."

John spoke highly of the "beloved Gaius," to whom the letter is addressed, commending him as a man who walks in truth, and supports missionaries. In contrast, he warns the church about Diotrephes, who has a reputation for being spiritually proud, not welcoming traveling missionaries, refusing to accept John's letter, and spreading malicious gossip. Diotrephes was power hungry and motivated by ego, and actually excommunicated those who reached out to help those sent out.

Finally, John mentioned Demetrius as another good example to emulate, because he was well spoken of by everyone, and "from the truth itself." Even the disciples agreed to "bear witness" to his good testimony.

In these fourteen verses we get a good picture of what "finishing well" looks like. In our text verse, the elderly John writes to Gaius and the other believers in expressions of love and sincere affection. "I have no greater joy," he says, "than to hear that my children walk in truth." He loves them as if they were his own children!

When I became a Christian, I was single. I had never experienced being a father. The joy that accompanied my salvation was exciting, wonderful, and very fulfilling. A little over a year

*When the Lord Rejoices* 139

later, I met my bride and we were married. More joy! Two years later, we became parents. I became the father of a son—then two sons. The tremendous joy I experienced while facing the many challenges of fatherhood added to an already rich life. Three years later, the Lord put me into full time ministry and I was ordained as a minister of the Gospel. I became a pastor. I had been given the opportunity to teach the Scriptures and disciple people in the faith.

Great joy fills my heart when I see and hear people walking strong in the faith! As a father of biological children, I rejoice when they do well, especially in the Lord! As a spiritual father to others, I also experience great joy when they are strong in the faith.

Pay attention to this very closely. This understanding can give you a better comprehension of how the Lord rejoices when you are walking in the truth. The Lord is a Father of many children. He knows each of us intimately by name. When a believer responds to His love and applies the Word to his life, the Lord rejoices. When a believer submits to God's will with a surrender of his own free will, the Lord's heart swells with joy.

There was a time in my life when I thought God was a faceless, supreme being, a law giver, and an enforcer, using the threat of hell to get men to believe. I was young and knew very little about spiritual matters. I became a born again Christian at age 28. Someone told me that God died for my sins and He wanted to have a personal relationship with me. I had come to the end all hope, and couldn't go on living the way I was. My life was miserable when I finally cried out for God to save me.

In a moment, I experienced an assurance of my sins being forgiven and of a new nature given to me. I began to read the Bible and discovered the true nature of my God. He is a Father, full of compassion and mercy, holy, righteous, sovereign, desiring a relationship with me. In this walk of faith, He wants me to "finish well." He has given me the Holy Spirit to empower me to "finish well."

As you meditate on these first four verses of 3 John, think of them in the context of your heavenly Father speaking to you as a son or daughter. John spoke to Gaius as a pastor and a brother. I pray that you will experience this joy in both positions. That your joy will be full as you disciple others, and that your joy will be full as you please the Father with your walk of faith today.

140   *Press On: 52 Reasons to Stay in the Race*

# WEEK FORTY-THREE
## *Who Is the Paul In Your Life?*

### Call of God, Timothy

*"God, who has saved us and called us with a holy calling, not according to our works, but according to His own purpose and grace which was given to us in Christ Jesus before time began, but has now been revealed by the appearing of our Savior Jesus Christ, who has abolished death and brought life and immortality to light through the gospel, to which I was appointed a preacher, an apostle, and a teacher of the Gentiles.—**2 Timothy 1:9-11***

At a recent men's retreat, we were challenged by three questions:
- Who is the "Paul" in your life? (Someone to learn from.)
- Who is the "Barnabas" in your life? (Someone who encourages us.)
- Who is the "Timothy" in your life? (Someone we can disciple.)[17]

As I thought about these questions, I read through Paul's letters to Timothy, and was struck by the passage above from Paul's second letter to his young son in the faith. Timothy began to travel and minister with the apostle as a very young man (possibly a teenager), during Paul's second missionary journey. This was probably the final letter of Paul's life, since we know he was executed by the Roman emperor Nero not long after it was written (64 AD).

Timothy was feeling discouraged and ill. Some of the older folks were finding it difficult to listen and learn from such a young pastor and made his youth an issue. Paul, wanting to encourage and strengthen Timothy, reminded his young friend to "stir up" the gifts that were given to him by the Holy Spirit by the laying on of hands, and of the calling upon his life.

We all need to be reminded occasionally of our callings. Doubt, misgiving, fatigue, trials, distractions, discouragement—the enemy tries many tactics to undermine what God wants to do in our lives. Sometimes it is the very people we are leading who challenge us because we're too young, or lack experience, or don't have the proper education, or...the list

*Who Is the Paul In Your Life?* 141

goes on. We can also misunderstand the call of God, thinking that we are somehow responsible for the fruitfulness of our ministry, rather than trusting the Lord to bring the harvest.

Paul reminds us of three things in verse nine of our text above:

- God has saved us and called us with a holy calling.
- It is not according to *our* works, but according to *His* purpose.
- Grace was given to us in Christ Jesus before time began.

By the end of this passage, Paul clearly defined the call upon his own life. He knew that he was appointed (ordained) a preacher, an apostle, and a teacher to the Gentiles, and he was determined to remain faithful to that calling. He wrote these letters from his heart, wanting Timothy to possess that same assurance of the nature of his calling.

When Paul wrote this letter he was in a Roman prison—and he knew that this too was part of what God had called him to, and he was not afraid or ashamed. Why? Because, as he said so eloquently, "I know *whom* I have believed and am persuaded that He is able to keep what is committed to Him until that Day" (2 Timothy 1:12). Our belief is in the person of Jesus Christ, not an ideology. Our faith is in the God of the Bible, not just the Bible. We can be secure in our calling, because we are secure in His ability to keep what we have committed until "that Day" when the Lord returns in power and glory.

As Paul addresses Timothy throughout this letter, it is heartwarming to see how he wrote about "us" and "we" and included Timothy in all his discussions of this wonderful call of God. Don't you feel strengthened when you are around people who encourage you in the faith and recognize God's call upon your life? It's also refreshing to be around people who are confident in God's call. Not in themselves, but in the assurance that God has called them to a certain task, vocation, lifestyle, or ministry. A few verses later in his letter, Paul asked for a blessing on the household of Onesiphorus, someone Paul found "refreshing" because he understood Paul's imprisonment and encouraged his ministry.

It is essential for us to be secure in who we are in Christ, because only then can we resist being intimidated by people's opinions and criticisms. When we are secure in God's call upon our lives, we are not as prone to fall for the devil's mind games or attacks upon our ministry. We are less defensive and

142   *Press On: 52 Reasons to Stay in the Race*

less threatened by other brothers and sisters and their gifts. This is the mindset Paul taught and encouraged in Timothy throughout his letters.

I think a lot about those three questions. About who teaches me, encourages me, and who I can in turn teach and encourage as we all seek to live the lives God wants for us. I pray that you will stop and ask yourself these three questions, and then pray for God to bring you someone to fill those positions in your life.

May you find security and assurance in your call and your position in Christ today.

"I'd rather have people hate me with the knowledge that I tried to save them."

Keith Green

# WEEK FORTY-FOUR
## *Answered Prayer from a Helpless Vessel*

### *Vision*

*And now I urge you to take heart, for there will be no loss of life among you, but only of the ship. For there stood by me this night an angel of the God to whom I belong and whom I serve, saying, "Do not be afraid, Paul; you must be brought before Caesar; and indeed God has granted you all those who sail with you."*

*Therefore take heart, men, for I believe God that it will be just as it was told me. However, we must run aground on a certain island."*—**Acts 27:22 -26**

Take heart. When you desperately need a vision from God, take heart. As you live your life and face big dramatic storms, or just wade your way through daily details that need your constant attention, expect God to give you a vision for your life and ministry.

We tend to think of spiritual visions taking place during a church service, or a prayer meeting, but biblically, most visions occur in the course of daily life. Sometimes it happens during a crisis, when desperation opens our spiritual eyes. In this chapter in the Book of Acts, Paul, a Roman prisoner, was escorted to Rome by a Roman centurion. They traveled on a civilian ship and soon ran into trouble.

This whole chapter would be a great script for an action packed sea adventure. Remember *Poseidon Adventure* (1972, remade 2006), about a cruise liner capsized at sea by a huge wave? The hero in that movie is a backslidden priest who finds the courage to save his fellow passengers. *The Perfect Storm* (2000) about a fishing vessel caught between two huge storms that converge in the North Atlantic Ocean is another sea thriller. The captain and all the crew are lost when giant waves overwhelm the tiny vessel. Hollywood's skillful special effects make the action seem so real. I felt like I was in the middle of those disasters—powerful human dramas that most times have *human* heroes.

But in the biblical stories, the hero is God working through a human vessel. Today in Bible colleges across the country students are being exhorted to become "visionaries" and to develop a vision for reaching the last generation. There are programs to help the believer become "purpose driven" and chart the course for their ministry. While this might be productive, it feels manufactured. In contrast, the vision Paul experienced during this voyage was the kind of vision that manifests itself as a sovereign act of God, through the gifts of the Holy Spirit—an answered prayer from a helpless vessel.

Paul and everyone aboard this ship were at the mercy of a storm called *Euroclydon*, defined as, "a strong southeast wind that stirs up broad waves," or in a term familiar to people who live by the sea, a strong "northeaster." Having seen those movies, I can at least imagine the terror of being caught in such an immense storm! The crew struck the sails, battened down the hatches, and held on for dear life, having lost all control of the ship. They saw neither the sun nor stars for days and nights, and as the storm raged they grew resigned to not making it out alive. Paul's companion, Luke, wrote, "...all hope that we would be saved was finally given up" (verse 20).

They gave up. They stopped eating, quit trying to fight, and waited for the end. Then, after a long time without food, Paul stood up in the midst of this weary and desolate crew and spoke the words of this week's text. Reread it slowly and let what Paul is saying really sink in.

"Take heart, have courage," he said, because the Lord had given him a vision. I love the verse where he speaks of the angel sent by the God, *"to whom I belong and whom I serve."* We belong to God! He bought us with the price of His blood. He is faithful to watch over those who are His. The God we serve is a living God whose hand is not too short to save!

Then Paul revealed what the angel said to him in the midst of the storm: "Do not be afraid, Paul; you must be brought before Caesar, and indeed God has granted you all those who sail with you." We are invincible until it is our time to go. The Lord holds us in His hand and no one can touch us, unless He grants permission. Finally, Paul repeated his words of encouragement: "Therefore take heart (courage) men, for I believe God that it will be just as it was told me." The Lord gave Paul a vision coupled with prophecy. What a powerful message of hope in the midst of life threatening circumstances!

Has life dealt you a blow that you are certain will be the end of you? Do you believe that God will get you through the situation you are in right now? Just when all hope is given up, and you can't see the sun or the stars, may the Lord gives you a vision of hope and encouragement. May He open your eyes today to see the salvation of your God.

"A church in the land without the Spirit is rather a curse than a blessing. If you have not the Spirit of God, Christian worker, remember that you stand in somebody else's way; you are a fruitless tree standing where a fruitful tree might grow."

Charles Spurgeon

# WEEK FORTY-FIVE
## Washed and Set Apart for His Use

### Faithfulness of God

*Now may the God of peace Himself sanctify you completely; and may your whole spirit, soul, and body be preserved blameless at the coming of our Lord Jesus Christ. He who calls you is faithful, who also will do it.*
**—1 Thessalonians 5:23-24**

The pastors and elders of our church pray for people at the front of the church after the service. One of the most common prayer requests comes from believers who continually struggle with sin and fear that they will never be completely sanctified, much less "preserved blameless" when the Lord returns. They are wracked with guilt and condemnation. The old nature persistently tries to rise up and take over once again. How can we ever be blameless?

Sanctification is an ongoing work of the Holy Spirit. And while to many people the word "sanctification" sounds very lofty and theological, it basically means that God is preparing us and setting us apart to be used by Him.

Paul's first letter to the Thessalonians is in response to Timothy's good report of their extensive ministry to the Gentiles, in 51 AD. Paul was only there about three weeks and was forced to leave under pressure from the Jews. In this letter Jesus is presented as the believers hope of salvation, and the prospect of His return is a comfort to those suffering from persecution or hardships.

Paul taught five things Jesus will do when He returns: He will deliver us from the wrath to come (1:10), reward the believer (1:19), perfect the believer (3:13), resurrect the believer, (4:13-18), and lastly, sanctify the believer (5:23-24, this week's text). Paul closed the letter with this beautiful prayer and a statement of God's faithfulness. He prayed that the God of peace, Himself, would set us apart, completely, sanctifying us through the ongoing work of the Holy Spirit.

Below are some of the Scriptures that speak of this sanctification:

*"Peter, an apostle of Jesus Christ...elect according to the foreknowledge of God the Father, in sanctification of the Spirit, for obedience and sprinkling of the blood of Jesus Christ: Grace to you and peace be multiplied."—1 Peter 1:2*

*"But we are bound to give thanks to God always for you, brethren beloved by the Lord, because God from the beginning chose you for salvation through sanctification by the Spirit and belief in the truth..." 2 Thessalonians 2:13*

Sanctification is a work of the Spirit, also accomplished through the Word of God, as mentioned in the prayer of Jesus in the Gospel of John: *"Sanctify them by Your truth. Your word is truth." — John 17:17*

After you are washed and set apart for His use, Paul prayed, "May your whole spirit, soul, and body be preserved blameless at the coming of our Lord Jesus Christ." What a wonderful prayer, and an awesome concept!

Then Paul, who knew what it meant to struggle with sin, who once cried out "O wretched man that I am!" —this same Paul now reminds us of the faithfulness of God: "He who calls you is faithful, who also will do it." Be sure to underline this verse in your Bible! The faithfulness of God declares that He will sanctify us and justify us by His Word and His Holy Spirit. It is not the impossible dream, but a fact. Our relationship to Jesus Christ has placed us in the heavenly realm. The giving of the Holy Spirit has assured us the strength to say no to sin and to have victory over the flesh.

The closer we draw to Jesus Christ, the more aware we become of our own depravity. And sometimes those in the ministry, feeling a deep sense of responsibility, struggle with feelings of inadequacy. Charles H. Spurgeon, once described as "the prince of preachers,"[18] often struggled with his sense of spiritual poverty. When large crowds came to hear him preach, he wanted to run into the forest and hide. He also continually fought against his pride. He specifically asked people to not compliment him, even when his oratory soared and he delivered a great message. He said it was like heaping logs upon a fire.[19] But oh how thankful Spurgeon was that our God is faithful, and He will sanctify us so that our whole spirit, soul, and body will be preserved blameless when He returns.

This is a work of the Spirit and not of our flesh. We can trust this work completely to Him; therefore, we can relax and follow our callings to serve Him until He comes. For that I am so grateful!

# WEEK FORTY-SIX
## *When the Righteous Suffer*

---

### *Perseverance*

---

*"As long as my breath is in me, and the breath of God in my nostrils, my lips will not speak wickedness, nor my tongue utter deceit. Far be it from me that I should say you are right; till I die I will not put away my integrity from me. My righteousness I hold fast, and will not let it go; my heart shall not reproach me as long as I live."* —**Job 27:3-6**

Job's friends offered him bad counsel and an even worse friendship. They decided that Job's numerous sins had brought God's judgment upon him. His good "friend" Bildad even called him a maggot and a worm (chapter 25).

Job lost everything. His property burned. His children died tragically. Boils afflicted his body from the top of his head to the soles of his feet. His reputation suffered. But Job persevered through his trials day by day, even though his wife turned against him, and his friends harshly criticized him.

Job emerged from these horrors as a rare man, committed to remaining faithful to his God, to maintaining his integrity, and to holding fast to righteousness. Job's perspective and his view of God remained consistent. He saw God as a big God, omnipotent, omniscient, faithful, merciful, righteous, and sovereign.

Pushed beyond what most of us could endure, badgered by critics, suffering from pain and heartache, Job answered his critics, summing up his position in one of the most profound statements ever recorded: **"Though He slay me, yet will I trust Him"** (Job 13:15). I remember reading those words for the first time. I had never met anyone in my life who had this kind of strength and commitment to anything. I felt like I had at last met a man who believed in something bigger than him, something beyond this physical life and this world. I grew to learn that Job's ability to press on, to persevere in the face of such tragedy, was strengthened by his knowledge and understanding of God. I have prayed ever since for the Lord to give me that kind of faith and commitment.

We have a tendency to think that such confidence in God

*When the Righteous Suffer* 151

is rewarded by safety and security, that God will surely provide blessing and deliverance from the loss of life in exchange for faithful belief. But we live in a fallen world where death and illness befall us. Our confidence is often mistakenly placed in that perception of safety. Job's confidence was in God and His character and nature. Job trusted God to know what the outcome should be, and willingly surrendered his future to the Lord. We need to remember that the Lord always works with an eternal perspective. "Though He slay me, yet will I trust Him," Job was able to say. How? Because even if he died, he trusted God for the future.

Eliphaz, the Temanite, one of Job's friends, accused him of backsliding and needing to "acquaint" himself with the Lord and His instructions. "Lay up His words in your heart," Eliphaz suggested (22:22).

Job had done more than "acquaint" himself with the Lord. "He knows me," Job responded. "When He has tested me, I shall come forth as gold. My foot has held fast to His steps; I have kept His way and not turned aside. I have not departed from the commandment of His lips; I have treasured the words of His mouth more than my necessary food" (23:10-12).

This was a man strengthened by God's Word, and living with an eternal perspective. I want that in my life, the ability to be so confident in God, that I stop worrying about my life here on earth. I have never suffered in my Christian walk as Job suffered. I have experienced tragedy and deep heartache, but my life has also been blessed in many ways since I became a Christian. Sometimes I wonder how I would do if I ever had to suffer for my faith.

In July of 1989, I traveled to China with a small team of seven. We were able to visit a small house church and the pastor, Samuel Lamb, in the city of Guangzhou in mainland China. Pastor Lamb was arrested in 1958 during to the cultural revolution of Mao Se Tung, charged with the crime of being a minister of the Gospel. He spent twenty years in prison, working in a coal mine connecting coal cars. Having committed several of Paul's letters to memory before his arrest, he testifies that the Word of God kept him strong through those twenty years of hardship. Chairman Mao died in 1976, and the revolution was over. Pastor Lamb was released in 1978.

I try to imagine myself spending twenty years in such desperate circumstances, and pray for strength. It was such a privilege to meet and talk with Pastor Lamb. When I asked him how I could be a better pastor, he said that following Jesus under persecution was difficult, but following Jesus in a comfortable, affluent place was harder. He encouraged me to persevere in teaching people to walk with Jesus in spite of our culture.

Job's attitude was that as long as he had the breath of God in him, he would not speak wickedness. He would hold fast to righteousness and never let it go. Pastor Lamb's attitude was that he gladly suffered with the people of God, rather than enjoy the temporary pleasures of sin (Hebrews 11:25).

Let us press on and learn from these men of God. May our faith grow and may our resolve be set to serve Him, no matter what the circumstances, until He comes.

*"I love to live on the brink of eternity."*

*David Brainerd*

# WEEK FORTY-SEVEN
## Remembering the Promise of God

### *Reality of God*

*And Abraham said to his young men, "Stay here with the donkey; the lad and I will go yonder and worship, and we will come back to you." So Abraham took the wood of the burnt offering and laid it on Isaac his son; and he took the fire in his hand, and a knife, and the two of them went together. But Isaac spoke to Abraham his father and said, "My father!" And he said, "Here I am, my son." Then he said, "Look, the fire and the wood, but where is the lamb for a burnt offering?" And Abraham said, "My son, God will provide for Himself the lamb for a burnt offering."*

*So the two of them went together. Then they came to the place of which God had told him. And Abraham built an altar there and placed the wood in order; and he bound Isaac his son and laid him on the altar, upon the wood. And Abraham stretched out his hand and took the knife to slay his son.*

*But the Angel of the Lord called to him from heaven and said, "Abraham, Abraham!" So he said, "Here I am." And He said, "Do not lay your hand on the lad, or do anything to him; for now I know that you fear God, since you have not withheld your son, your only son, from Me."*

*Then Abraham lifted his eyes and looked, and there behind him was a ram caught in a thicket by its horns. So Abraham went and took the ram, and offered it up for a burnt offering instead of his son. And Abraham called the name of the place, The-Lord-Will-Provide; as it is said to this day, "In the Mount of The Lord it shall be provided."*

*Then the Angel of the Lord called to Abraham a second time out of heaven, and said: "By Myself I have sworn, says the Lord, because you have done this thing, and have not withheld your son, your only son— blessing I will bless you, and multiplying I will multiply your descendants as the stars of the heaven and as the sand which is on the seashore; and your descen-*

*Remembering the Promise of God* 155

*dants shall possess the gate of their enemies. In your seed all the nations of the earth shall be blessed, because you have obeyed My voice." So Abraham returned to his young men, and they rose and went together to Beersheba; and Abraham dwelt at Beersheba.* **—Genesis 22:5-19**

This story has always astounded me. Abraham had his faults and human weaknesses, like when he suffered a lapse of faith in Egypt during the famine. In a moment of cowardice and fear, he told Sarai, his wife, to lie to King Abimelech and tell him she was his sister. This was technically true in that she was Abraham's half sister, but not in light of their real relationship as husband and wife. He also managed to add the Egyptian handmaiden, Hagar, to his household during this incident (Genesis 12:10). Abraham was not a shining example of courage and faith at that time!

But now, many years later, "the friend of God" had grown into a man full of faith, who responded immediately to God's instructions. He completely trusted God, for the Lord had kept every promise and led Abraham through many perilous and difficult times.

Abraham and Sara waited for twenty-five years for this son to be born. Ten years after the promise, Sara grew impatient and gave her handmaiden, Hagar, to Abraham, hoping to give him a son, trying on her own to fulfill God's promise. Ishmael was the fruit of that decision, and the consequences are still being felt today. The descendents of Ishmael (the Arab nations), the son of the flesh, are still warring with the descendents of Isaac (the Jewish nation), the son of the promise from God.

When God asked the unthinkable, Abraham responded in a powerful demonstration of faith. He obeyed the God who had spoken to him in a familiar and unmistakable voice, calling his name. I am always astounded by Abraham's faith and obedience when I think of the son, miraculously born to a ninety-nine year old father and a ninety-year old mother, who was the fulfillment of a promise of God. Through this son, "I will make you exceedingly fruitful; and I will make nations of you, and kings shall come from you," God promised (Genesis 17:6)!

My human, rational mind, in that situation, would've said, "Why would God tell me sacrifice the son we waited so long for? How will God fulfill His promise if this son is dead? How could He ask this of me?" My intellect would've screamed, "No! This cannot be God!"

But Abraham obeyed without hesitation, without questioning. He did not consult his wife. He did not run or try to figure it out in his mind. Through the rest of Abraham's life story, and many centuries later after the birth of the Church, we get a glimpse into why Abraham was capable of such obedience. "By faith," the book of Hebrews tells us, "Abraham...offered up Isaac...concluding that God was able to raise him up, even from the dead..." (Hebrews 11:17-19). Abraham lived in the reality of God! God was not just a figurative, supreme being to whom he was subservient. To Abraham, God was real, and able to fulfill *all* His the promises, even if it meant raising Isaac from the dead.

Abraham had such confidence in the reality of God that he could live by the words, "God said it, I believe it, that settles it!" I don't know who is responsible for that quote but I think it applies here. When God's command flies in the face of everything logical, reasonable, practical, or rational, we need to step out and obey. This is the reality of God.

There is a game that father's play with their children. The father places the child on the side of a swimming pool while he stands in the water close to the middle of the pool. The father extends his arms and calls to the child to jump. The child leaps into the father's arms, laughing with childish glee, knowing and trusting the father to be there with open arms. The child has no fear because the father is big, strong, able to hold him, and has promised to be there!

Why do we hesitate and resist when our heavenly Father calls to us from the midst of circumstance with His arms extended? Why do we doubt His ability to hold us up and get us through the darkest night, or the deepest financial waters? It is because He is not real to us but rather, a spiritual apparition. C.H. Spurgeon once said, "How can we say we trust God with our eternal destiny, when we question His ability to save us from our day to day problems?"[20]

May we follow Abraham's example of trusting in the reality of God today!

*Remembering the Promise of God* 157

"Is prayer your steering wheel or your spare tire?"

*Corrie Ten Boom*

# WEEK FORTY-EIGHT
## Why We Build Memorials

### Answers to Prayer

*Joshua said to them: "Cross over before the ark of the Lord your God into the midst of the Jordan, and each one of you take up a stone on his shoulder, according to the number of the tribes of the children of Israel, that this may be a sign among you when your children ask in time to come, saying, 'What do these stones mean to you?' Then you shall answer them that the waters of the Jordan were cut off before the ark of the covenant of the Lord; when it crossed over the Jordan, the waters of the Jordan were cut off. And these stones shall be for a memorial to the children of Israel forever."*
**–Joshua 4:5-7**

On the overflowing eastern bank of the Jordan River, the nation of Israel—over two million people and their herds of cattle and sheep—waited to cross. On the other side, the Promised Land awaited. Now all they needed was a way across—and the Lord was about to provide it.

Joshua gathered his people and told them, "Come here, and hear the words of the Lord your God...By this you shall know that the living God is among you...Behold, the ark of the covenant of the Lord of all the earth is crossing over before you into the Jordan...as soon as the soles of the feet of the priests who bear the ark of the Lord, the Lord of all the earth, shall rest in the waters of the Jordan, that the waters of the Jordan shall be cut off" (Joshua 3). Just as the Lord parted the Red Sea for the children of Israel forty years before, now, on the tenth day of Nisan, He would part the Jordan River as they finally entered the Promised Land.

As soon as the priests stepped into the river, the waters ceased their natural flow, and dry ground allowed the people to cross. The Lord instructed Joshua to have a man from each tribe pick a stone from the dry riverbed, take it to their campsite on the other side, and use the stones to build a memorial to commemorate this day.

The Lord also told Joshua to pile another twelve stones in the midst of the river while the waters were parted. The priests

*Why We build Memorials* 159

were to remain in the midst of the parted waters until every one of the children of Israel crossed over the river. When everyone crossed, and the twelve stones were piled up, the priests walked out of the riverbed, carrying the Ark of the Covenant. As soon as the soles of their feet touched dry land, the waters returned and overflowed the banks.

This was the day the children of Israel had been waiting to see for many, many years. An answer to prayer, and a testimony of the power and faithfulness of God, this day has long since been remembered and celebrated as one of the most significant dates in Jewish history.

The memorial was built, Joshua explained, so that "When your children ask in time to come, saying, 'What do these stones mean to you?'" there will be an opportunity to glorify the Lord. "That all the peoples of the earth may know the hand of the Lord, that it is mighty, that you may fear the Lord your God forever."

In our Christian walk, we will face many challenges in which the Lord will work in sometimes quiet, sometimes miraculous ways. We'll see many answers to many prayers, but unfortunately, with the passing of time, we too easily forget how He provided for us in times of need, or delivered us from harm or fear. We are like the children of Israel in that respect. When they grew weary or faced new trials, they forgot that God had miraculously delivered them from Egypt. They forgot the many ways God provided for them and protected them during forty years of wandering in the desert. They even forget about God.

We read those stories and wonder—what were they thinking? How could they forget the Red Sea and manna from heaven? But we do the same thing today! Stress, worry, fatigue, and the trials of life distract us and we forget how God provided miraculously, or healed our body or a loved one. We might even go days without thinking of God at all!

That's why we make memorials. To remind us of God's faithfulness and power. Memorials are usually made of stone or wood. But many of our memorials are an underlined Bible verse, a date written in the margin, or an entry in a prayer journal. When you open your Bible or your journal, these words pierce your heart as memorials to answered prayers, and provoke us to practice the presence of the living God.

When you come into my office you will immediately see a pictorial memorial of sorts. Pictures of people and places,

160    *Press On: 52 Reasons to Stay in the Race*

connected to an event, a ministry, or a special moment in my life, remind me of answered prayers and the faithfulness and power of God. This helps me to remember the God to whom I belong, and whom I serve.

May I encourage you to mark your Bible when God answers a specific prayer, and keep some kind of a prayer journal, so that you can look back and be reminded of the protection and provision of God in your life. Then, when you are on your deathbed, and entering into glory, you can leave behind a memorial that others can read, and know *"...the hand of the Lord, that it is mighty, that you may fear the Lord your God forever."*

"Courage is contagious. When a brave man takes a stand, the spines of others are stiffened."

Billy Graham

# WEEK FORTY-NINE
## Young and in Captivity

---

### *Finishing Well*

*Although I heard, I did not understand. Then I said, "My lord, what shall be the end of these things?" And he said, "Go your way, Daniel, for the words are closed up and sealed till the time of the end. Many shall be purified, made white, and refined, but the wicked shall do wickedly; and none of the wicked shall understand, but the wise shall understand. And from the time that the daily sacrifice is taken away, and the abomination of desolation is set up, there shall be one thousand two hundred and ninety days. Blessed is he who waits, and comes to the one thousand three hundred and thirty-five days. But you, go your way till the end; for you shall rest, and will arise to your inheritance at the end of the days."*
**—Daniel 12:8-13**

King Nebuchadnezzar was very specific about the kinds of young men he intended to kidnap during his raid of Jerusalem:

*"Then the king instructed Ashpenaz, the master of his eunuchs, to bring some of the children of Israel and some of the king's descendants and some of the nobles, young men in whom there was no blemish, but good-looking, gifted in all wisdom, possessing knowledge and quick to understand, who had ability to serve in the king's palace, and whom they might teach the language and literature of the Chaldeans"* (Daniel 1:3-4).

In three separate raids, around 606 B.C., the Babylonian army plundered Jerusalem and captured Daniel and other intelligent, promising young men, specifically to train them to serve the king. Daniel was probably about sixteen years old.

This must have been a pretty horrifying experience if you think about it. Your city is invaded, robbed, and all the best and brightest young men are carried away from their families and homes. A very hard place for a young man to find himself.

But God had a plan for Daniel's life: he was destined to become a prophetic witness to the Jewish and Gentile world. Daniel ultimately spent seventy years in captivity, serving God in a secular and pagan court, and became a powerful witness to the sovereignty of the God of Abraham, Isaac, and Jacob. This one young man dramatically impacted an entire kingdom!

And, Daniel finished well. He spent a lifetime serving God, in both prosperity and adversity. As a teenager, he demonstrated great faith and strength of character when he refused to eat the king's meat or drink. God blessed him by giving Daniel "understanding in all visions and dreams" (1:17). Seventy-five percent of the book of Daniel revolves around visions and dreams.

Isn't it wonderful to see a teenager anointed by the hand of God and placed in a position of such important service? Isn't it wonderful to see a faithful witness who endured for seventy years, not marred by scandal or backsliding?

My Christian walk began when I was twenty-eight years old. I went from captivity to freedom when I met Jesus Christ. Now, I have been walking with Jesus for over thirty years. Compared to Daniel, I'm still a new Christian. Finishing well is a passion of my heart, and I hope of yours as well.

There was a time when I thought I could not serve God in a secular job. I wanted to be in the ministry, on staff at a healthy, thriving church. I know that some Christians believe the secret to having a strong Christian walk is to be in a totally Christian environment. But that's wrong! Look at Daniel. The secret to having a strong Christian walk is to have a close personal relationship with Jesus. *It is not the environment that determines our walk.*

Daniel went from freedom to captivity; from Jerusalem, the site of his faith, to Babylon; from religious freedom to persecution. He spent a lifetime being exposed to secular, pagan idolatry, yet he remained faithful to the God he worshiped.

Many strong leaders have impacted our world with their philosophy. Karl Marx, the father of Communism; Adolf Hitler, the perpetrator of Nazi Germany; Mao Se Tung, whose influence still affects a billion Chinese on the planet earth. They aimed their philosophies toward the youth. They knew that if they could capture the hearts and minds of the youth, their nations would embrace their teachings.

Young people are vulnerable, but Daniel's example demonstrates the power of the living God to keep young men and women strong in their faith—for a lifetime! Through the power of the Holy Spirit, God gives all of us—men and women, young and old alike—the capacity to remain strong and finish well.

Read Daniel 12:8-13 in your Bible, and underline the parts that minister to you today. This is a promise to all of us who are serving God. We have an incorruptible inheritance awaiting us. We have the omnipotent God within us to enable us to serve Him in this secular, pagan, and fallen world. I pray that today you will find encouragement to stay the course, press on, and finish well.

"Each time, before you intercede, be quiet first, and worship God in His glory."

Andrew Murray

# WEEK FIFTY

## "I Know You By Name"

### *Faithfulness of God*

*Then Moses said to the Lord, "See, You say to me, 'Bring up this people.' But You have not let me know whom You will send with me. Yet You have said, 'I know you by name, and you have also found grace in My sight.' Now therefore, I pray, if I have found grace in Your sight, show me now Your way, that I may know You and that I may find grace in Your sight. And consider that this nation is Your people."*

*And He said, "My Presence will go with you, and I will give you rest."*

*Then he said to Him, "If Your Presence does not go with us, do not bring us up from here. For how then will it be known that Your people and I have found grace in Your sight, except You go with us? So we shall be separate, Your people and I, from all the people who are upon the face of the earth."*

*So the Lord said to Moses, "I will also do this thing that you have spoken; for you have found grace in My sight, and I know you by name."*

*And he said, "Please, show me Your glory."*

*Then He said, "I will make all My goodness pass before you, and I will proclaim the name of the Lord before you. I will be gracious to whom I will be gracious, and I will have compassion on whom I will have compassion." But He said, "You cannot see My face; for no man shall see Me, and live." And the Lord said, "Here is a place by Me, and you shall stand on the rock. So it shall be, while My glory passes by, that I will put you in the cleft of the rock, and will cover you with My hand while I pass by. Then I will take away My hand, and you shall see My back; but My face shall not be seen."—Exodus 33:12-23*

I love this text and I pray that it becomes a favorite of yours as well, because it clearly portrays the reality and the faithfulness of our God.

Moses was a very real, down-to-earth, complex individual.

He was also a great example of spiritual leadership because he wasn't afraid to be real. He was afraid, however, of the monumental task put before him, and he voiced his concerns to God in a series of reverent, but honest conversations.

This is a lesson for all of us. We must always be honest with God, never forgetting His character or His nature. And, like Moses, we need to recognize that the strength of spiritual leadership is to be God-dependent and not self-sufficient.

Moses asked God two things. First, as he prepared to leave Mt. Sinai, with a nation of people who had just grievously disobeyed the Lord and fallen into idolatry, he asked for the assurance that God would still go with them. Second, Moses asked to see God's glory.

Notice in the dialogue above how Moses repeats back to God what he believes God told him. This is a great tool for good communication. When talking with someone, repeating back what you think you heard helps confirm or clarify what was said. Moses wanted to be sure he understood what God said, and God reaffirms Moses, *"I know you by name, and you have found grace in My sight."* In verse fourteen, God says, *"My Presence will go with you and I will give you rest."*

Moses had to be sure that they were walking in grace (after all, they had just sinned and incurred God's wrath with the golden calf incident), and that God was going with him. Otherwise, he didn't want to go! It would just be too dangerous and impossible.

What a great lesson for us. When faced with the impossible, or the terrifying, or whatever daunting task comes our way, we don't need to be afraid to clarify the Lord's will in the situation. And, we don't have to worry about asking Him to confirm and *reaffirm* what we believe He said, to make it clear in our hearts. If I'm not sure God is going with me, like Moses, I don't want to go!

Now, Moses had already been respectfully honest with the Lord, extracting from Him a promise to go with them. But Moses wasn't satisfied. He wanted more. More of God. He asked a question that should encourage us as well to want more of God. "Please," he said, "show me Your glory."

So much is revealed in this dialogue about the nature and attributes of God, beginning with His willingness to engage in such an intimate, personal conversation. He explained to Moses that it is impossible for man see God face-to-face and live. Our corrupt carnal nature cannot behold the incorruptible holy God. However, God made a way to grant Moses his request.

God placed Moses in a crevice of a rock, then covered him with His own hand. As God passed by, Moses witnessed the trailing edge of His glory! Moses beheld the glory of the living God! Moses came down from the mountain forty days later, with his face literally shining, so much so that at first Aaron and the others were afraid to go near him!

God was not obligated to answer this request of Moses. But because of His faithfulness, God chose to make a way for Moses to behold His glory. While no man can literally see God's face and live, we know that Moses did have regular, "face-to-face" conversations with the Lord, as one would converse with a friend (Deuteronomy 34:10). Moses was not some nameless subject in God's kingdom. "I know you by name," God said.

Moses saw God's glory as mere reflection. As the apostle Paul wrote centuries later, "For now we see in a mirror, dimly, but then face to face" (1 Corinthians 13:12). Someday, we will be able see God face to face, in our new bodies, and join Moses and countless others gone before us, as we behold His glory. But until then, He gives us a way to experience His glory through the Holy Spirit, and to know Him, face to face, through His son, Jesus Christ, "the image of the invisible God" (Colossians 1:13-15) and "the brightness of His glory and the express image of His person" (Hebrews 1:3). The Son reveals the glory of God, and the Holy Spirit reveals the Son.

I pray that we can be like Moses, in our honesty with God, and our passion to be in His presence. May God hide us in the rock of Christ, cover us with His hand, and let us see His glory! And may our countenances be changed so that all around us can see that God is real!

"No matter how bad it gets here on earth, it is just temporary - and it beats hell!"

*Jon Courson*

# WEEK FIFTY-ONE
## *Trusting in the Mercy of God*

---

### *Answers to Prayer*

---

*To the Chief Musician. A Psalm of David the servant of the Lord, who spoke to the Lord the words of this song on the day that the Lord delivered him from the hand of all his enemies and from the hand of Saul. And he said: I will love You, O Lord, my strength. The Lord is my rock and my fortress and my deliverer; My God, my strength, in whom I will trust; My shield and the horn of my salvation, my stronghold. I will call upon the Lord, who is worthy to be praised; so shall I be saved from my enemies. —Psalm 18:1-3*

For years, Saul, a murderous, mad, and jealous king, pursued David. David was forced to hide in caves, live on the run, and spent almost twenty years dodging the king's efforts to kill him. David even had numerous opportunities to strike King Saul, but he refrained, declaring once, "I will not stretch out my hand against my lord, for he is the Lord's anointed" (1 Samuel 24). He believed it was God's responsibility to deal with Saul.

The saga began during Saul's reign when the prophet Samuel came to the house of Jesse to anoint one of Jesse's eight sons King of Israel. In obedience to the Lord, Samuel anointed David, the youngest, most unlikely choice (1 Samuel 16). Soon after David's legendary confrontation with Goliath, people began to see him as a mighty warrior. Saul's son, Jonathan, became David's closest friend, even giving up his right to the throne. David's growing popularity threatened Saul, and made David a target for the king's insane jealousy. David wrote this psalm when the Lord delivered him from the hand of Saul. With a heart full of thanksgiving and worship, David declared the Lord to be his rock, his fortress, and his deliverer.

When we are faced with a horrible trial, and circumstances are against us, it's easy to become angry and bitter, which can distort our concept of God. David held onto his concept of God as his strength and deliverer. He clung to his faith in the God he worshiped. If we lose sight of God and His faithfulness,

*Trusting in the Mercy of God* 171

and begin to rely on our own strength, we become vulnerable to the enemy's lies. Satan wants us to doubt the provision and protection of God, and will attack us with this lie every day.

David's foundation was his solid belief that God heard his prayers, and is real. God was everything that kept him going: his strength, his shield, his stronghold, and his salvation. In the midst of the hardest circumstances, David cried to Him, called upon Him, served Him, and deemed Him worthy to be praised. And because of that, he was able to say with confidence, *"So shall I be saved from my enemies."*

This Psalm expresses David's relationship with the Lord beautifully, as does Psalm 13: "I have trusted in Your mercy; my heart shall rejoice in Your salvation. I will sing to the Lord, because He has dealt bountifully with me." We need to grab hold of those words and never let go! Trusting in the mercy of God will keep us from becoming angry and bitter. Keeping a joyful, thankful heart will help us rejoice because God has answered our prayers, and dealt bountifully with us! We deserve hell. We live under the curse of Adam, for we are all sinners, desperately wicked, and guilty. Yet God in His mercy chose to die in our place, and blot out all the ordinances against us, past, present, and future.

"God doesn't owe us anything. He has done it all for us. No matter how bad it gets here on earth, it is only temporary. No matter how bad our circumstances become, it beats Hell!" said Pastor Jon Courson in a message I will never forget.

We are saved from our enemies; we have God as our rock, fortress, and deliverer. He is worthy to be praised. We can return His love with hearts full of trust in His mercy. We too can sing to the Lord, because He has dealt bountifully with us! God ultimately gave David the victory in his trial with Saul, and God will give us victory in our trials as well.

May we see God in the proper perspective today, knowing that He hears and answers our prayers, as we occupy until He comes.

# WEEK FIFTY-TWO
## *Living in Victory!*

*But thanks be to God, who gives us the victory through our Lord Jesus Christ. — **1 Corinthians 15:57***

The journey through the year is now complete. Each week we have studied Scriptures in light of seven topics necessary to keep us in the race and help us live in victory.

As Christians, we fight not for victory but from a place of victory. Jesus accomplished everything necessary for our redemption. He defeated the devil and we have escaped our enemy's grasp. The race we run is to spread the good news of this wonderful truth to others who have not heard about or experienced the victory in Jesus.

When World War II was over, and the Nazis had been defeated, the allied forces invaded all the prison camps to set the prisoners free. Their mission was to liberate those held captive by an enemy that had been vanquished. Now, it is our mission to do the same, and we too can "Go into all the world and preach the Gospel to every creature" (Mark 16), knowing that we go in victory.

To help us remember this truth I have created a simple acrostic based on the word victory. I hope that it helps you to also remember that we are more than conquerors in this life, through the work of Christ.

Please look up each of these verses, underline them, and highlight them so that you can be reminded of the victory that is already ours. I pray that we will all serve Him until He comes for us, that we will remain firmly in His grip, and be compelled by His love to reach out to others. I pray that God will refresh you today as you run the race to the finish line.

*Living in Victory* 173

**V** "How **very, very, very**, much He loves me." Jesus Christ loves me enough to give Himself for me while I am still a sinner. ***Romans 5:8***

**I** "You are my God, I will exalt you." ***Psalm 118:1-7, 18***

**C** "Jesus **Christ**, my joy, my strength, I hide myself in you." ***Psalm 32:1-7***

**T** "The **testing** of our faith produces patience." ***James 1:2-12***

**O** "Who is he who **overcomes** the world but he who believes that Jesus Christ is the Son of God?" ***1 John 5:4-5***

**R** "...you **rejoice** with joy, inexpressible, and full of Glory." ***1 Peter 1:1-9***

**Y** "**Yes**, Lord, I surrender." This is the key to victory. ***Romans 8:1-39***

# EPILOGUE

On the night of January 9, 2007, devastating tragedy rocked our family. We suddenly lost our 23 year-old son, Nathan. Every day since that night we have clung to the Lord searching for direction and answers. Our lives will never be the same, but we know the Lord will heal our broken hearts. The Lord was faithful to give us Psalm 71 two days before this tragic loss, knowing we would need comfort in the weeks and months ahead. When this took place, our oldest son, Aaron, was engaged in fierce combat in the El Anbar province in Iraq. He is a marine engaged in Operation Iraqi Freedom. Our faith and peace were shaken to the very core of our being. Fortunately Aaron returned home safely to his wife and daughter on April 17, 2007.

This book is a work that began over six years ago, prompted by the Spirit of God, as a labor of love to encourage readers in their walk of faith. We must "press on" in this life and in the work the Lord has called us to complete. There will be many times when we feel that we cannot go on, but the Word of God, revealed to us by the empowering of the Spirit, spurs us on into the fray. In the gospel of John, chapter 16, verse 33, Jesus says, "These things I have spoken to you, that in Me you may have peace. In the world you will have tribulation; but be of good cheer, I have overcome the world." Be encouraged in the work and in the life God has called you. He will get you through.

"Blessed are the flexible, they shall not be broken."

Chuck Smith

# FOOTNOTES

1. Guiness, Os, The Call (Nashville, TN: Word Publishing) 1998, p. 29.

2. J. Oswald Sanders, Spiritual Leadership, (Chicago: Moody Press, 1994), p. 57.

3. Compiled by A.C. Brooks, Answers to Prayer, from George Mueller's Narratives, (Chicago: Moody Press, 1984).

4. Ramona Ministerial Assn, Ramona, CA 1986 – 2003, Calvary Chapel Ramona, 2004-present.

5. Ramona Crisis Pregnancy Center, founded in 1987, presently operating as Ramona Pregnancy Care Clinic.

6. Jerusalem Post, March 12, 1992, page 1.

7. Leadership meeting, North Park Theater, 1979.

8. Moody Science Classics, Red River of Life, VHS Video, 1988.

9. Murietta Conference Center, Missions Conference, Isaiah 44:3, January 8, 2004.

10. Spurgeon, Charles, All of Grace (Whitaker House, 1981, 1983) p. 22.

11. Smith, Chuck and Brooke, Tal, Harvest (Costa Mesa: Word for Today, 1993) p. 24.

12. C. Austin Miles, In the Garden, March 1912.

13. Oswald Chambers, My Utmost for His Highest, (Uhrichsville, OH: Barbour and Company, Inc, 1963) p. 10.

14. Mike Fay, Tom Coomes, As We Gather, Maranatha Music, 1981.

15. Barnes, Peter, Out of Darkness Into Light Ministries, (1978).

16. Murietta Conference Center, Missions Conference, II Samuel 23:8, January 8, 2003.

17. Mark Searle, Calvary Chapel of Escondido Men's Retreat, 2005.

18. The Prince of Preachers with Dr. Ken Connolly. (A documentary on the life of Charles H. Spurgeon. Santa Ana, CA: International Baptist Missions), 1994.

19. C.H. Spurgeon, Lectures to My Students, (Grand Rapids: Zondervan) p. 331.

20. C.H. Spurgeon, Morning and Evening Devotion, Evening, March 7, Psalm 118:8 (New Kinnsington, PA: Whitaker House) Revised, 2001, p. 147.